# Table of Contents

**Preface to *The Silicocene: A New Epoch in History*........................ 10**
    Introduction: Setting the Stage.............................................................. 11
        Defining the Silicocene: What is the Silicocene? ...................... 11
        The Anthropocene: Humanity's Impact on the Earth.............. 12
        Technology and Evolution: A Co-evolutionary Force............. 13
        Emerging Trends: AI, Biotechnology, and Sustainability....... 15
    A New Age of Responsibility ................................................................ 17
    Industrial Revolution to Digital Age: A Brief History of
    Humanity's Technological Evolution...................................................... 18
        The Industrial Revolution (Late 18th - Early 19th Century) ... 18
        Second Industrial Revolution (Late 19th - Early 20th Century)
        .................................................................................................................20
        The Digital Revolution (Late 20th Century)...............................22
        From the Internet to the Age of AI (21st Century)...................23
    A Continuous Evolution .........................................................................25
    Capitalism and Technology: How Hypercapitalism Shaped
    Technological Development, Exploitation of Natural
    Resources, and Inequality.......................................................................25
        The Rise of Capitalism and its Influence on Technology.......25
        The Shift to Hypercapitalism .........................................................26
        The Role of Technology in Exploiting Natural Resources......28
        Hypercapitalism and Inequality: The Technological Divide.29
    Environmental Consequences and the Climate Crisis: A Dive into
    How Our Advancements Led to the Current Ecological Crisis .....31
        From Industrialization to the Climate Crisis: The
        Environmental Costs of Progress .................................................31
        Fossil Fuels and Greenhouse Gas Emissions .............................31
        The Exploitation of Natural Resources and Ecological
        Collapse ................................................................................................33
        The Pressing Need for Change: Towards Sustainability
        and Regeneration .............................................................................35

Conclusion: The Urgency of Transformative Action ........................ 36
Defining the Shift: What Catalyzed the Transition to the Silicocene? .................................................................................................... 37
    A World at a Crossroads ..................................................................... 37
    Climate Collapse: The Catalyst for Change .................................. 38
    AI Breakthroughs: Reshaping Economics and Society ........... 39
    A Change in Societal Values: Toward Sustainability and Equity ........................................................................................................ 42
Role of AI and Advanced Technology: Redefining Economics, Labor, and Human Relationships .................................... 45
    AI and the Future of Economics ...................................................... 45
    The Redefinition of Labor in the Silicocene ............................... 47
    AI and Human Relationships: The Personal and the Ethical .......................................................................................................... 49
Conclusion: The Emergence of the Silicocene ................................... 51
Biotech and the New Ecology: How Bioengineering and Synthetic Biology Play Into Humanity's New Relationship with Nature ............................................................................................................. 52
    The Dawn of Bioengineering and Synthetic Biology .............. 52
    Living Cities and Biophilic Design: Integrating Nature into Urban Spaces ............................................................................... 53
    Restoration Technologies: Healing Ecosystems with Bioengineering ..................................................................................... 55
    The New Ecology: Human and Nature in Symbiosis .............. 57
Techno-Moral Dilemmas: Ethical Challenges Arising from the Integration of AI and Biotech into Human Life ........................ 59
    Introduction to Techno-Moral Dilemmas ................................... 59
    Autonomy and Human Enhancement: Redefining the Human Experience ........................................................................... 60
    AI Governance and the Challenge of Alignment ..................... 62
    Bioethics and the Limits of Genetic Engineering .................... 64
    The Challenge of Ecological Balance and Bioengineering ... 66
Conclusion: Navigating the Techno-Moral Landscape of the Silicocene ................................................................................................. 68
The Societal Transformation in the Silicocene ................................. 69

Post-Hypercapitalism: The Emergence of New Economic Models ... 69
- The Circular Economy: Regeneration and Sustainability at the Core ... 70
- The Gift Economy: Building a Society Based on Generosity and Reciprocity ... 72
- The Digital Commons: A Shared Knowledge Economy ... 74

Decentralization and Empowerment: Reshaping Power Structures in the Silicocene ... 76
- Blockchain: A Framework for Decentralized Governance and Trust ... 76
- Decentralized AI: Democratizing Intelligence and Decision-Making ... 78
- Localism: Empowering Communities and Building Resilience ... 80

Conclusion: The Societal Transformation of the Silicocene ... 81

The Future of Work: How Automation and AI May Lead to Universal Basic Income (UBI), Shorter Work Weeks, and Creativity-Focused Economies ... 82
- Introduction to the Future of Work in the Silicocene ... 82
- Automation and Job Displacement: The Challenges of the AI Revolution ... 83
- Universal Basic Income (UBI): A Safety Net for the Age of Automation ... 84
- Shorter Work Weeks: Rethinking Productivity and Well-Being ... 86
- Creativity-Focused Economies: Valuing Human Innovation and Expression ... 87
- Conclusion: The Future of Work in the Silicocene ... 88

Equity and Justice in the Silicocene: Ensuring Marginalized Communities Benefit from Technological Shifts ... 89
- Introduction: Equity and Justice in a Technologically Transformed World ... 89
- The Digital Divide: Ensuring Equal Access to Technology ... 90
- Algorithmic Bias: Addressing Discrimination in AI Systems . 91

- Access to Education and Healthcare: Bridging Gaps in Essential Services ... 93
- Community Empowerment: Building Inclusive and Participatory Systems ... 94
- Conclusion: Equity and Justice in the Silicocene ... 95

Political Structures in the Silicocene: Governance, Democracy, and Global Cooperation ... 96
- Introduction: The Transformation of Governance in the Silicocene ... 96
- Decentralized Governance: Empowering Communities through Blockchain and DAOs ... 97
- Digital Democracy: Technology-Enhanced Participation and Decision-Making ... 98
- AI-Driven Governance: Improving Decision-Making and Public Services ... 100
- Global Cooperation: Addressing Transnational Challenges in the Silicocene ... 101
- Conclusion: Political Structures in the Silicocene ... 103

Chapter 5: Harmonizing with Nature - The Age of Symbiosis ... 104
- The Solarpunk Vision: Eco-Cities, Living Architecture, and Sustainable Energy ... 105
  - 1. Eco-Cities: Urban Centers as Living Organisms ... 105
  - 2. Living Architecture: Buildings as Ecosystems ... 106
  - 3. Sustainable Energy: The Sun, Wind, and Beyond ... 107
- Regeneration of the Earth: Reversing the Damage of the Anthropocene ... 108
  - 1. Carbon Capture and Negative Emissions Technology ... 108
  - 2. Reforestation and Ecological Restoration ... 109
  - 3. Ocean Regeneration and Climate Mitigation ... 110
- The Global Ecological Consciousness: Shifting Values in the Silicocene ... 110
  - 1. Redefining Progress and Success ... 111
  - 1. Redefining Progress and Success (continued) ... 111
  - 2. The Role of Indigenous Knowledge ... 112
  - 3. Education and Ecological Literacy ... 113

AI as Caretaker of the Earth: Stewardship and Ecological Management ......................................................................... 114
    1. AI-Driven Ecosystem Management ........................................ 114
    2. AI and Resource Management .............................................. 115
    3. AI-Driven Biodiversity Conservation ...................................... 116
Conclusion: The Age of Symbiosis ................................................ 117
The Role of Communities in the Silicocene: Empowerment and Localized Stewardship ....................................................... 118
    1. The Decentralization of Power and Resources ................... 119
    2. Bioregionalism: Thriving Within Natural Boundaries ....... 120
    3. Community Science and Citizen-Led Ecological Restoration ......................................................................................... 121
The Ethics of AI in the Silicocene: Ensuring Alignment with Human and Ecological Values ............................................... 122
    1. AI Alignment with Ecological Goals ...................................... 123
    2. Guarding Against Technological Exploitation .................... 124
    3. The Future of Human-AI Relationships ............................... 124
Conclusion: A Collaborative Future for Humanity, Technology, and Nature ............................................................... 125
AI Alignment and Ethical Futures .................................................... 127
  What is AI Alignment? .................................................................. 127
    1. The Necessity of Alignment in the Silicocene ..................... 128
    2. The Value Alignment Problem .............................................. 128
    3. The Challenge of Generalization .......................................... 129
    4. The Future of AI Alignment ................................................... 130
  Challenges in Alignment: Risks of Unaligned AI ........................ 130
    1. Superintelligence and Control Issues .................................. 130
    2. The Problem of Value Misalignment ................................... 131
    3. The Risk of Autonomous AI Systems ................................... 132
    4. Existential Risks of AI .............................................................. 132
  AI and Human Collaboration: Augmenting Human Intelligence and Empathy ....................................................... 133
    1. AI as a Collaborative Partner ................................................. 133
    2. Enhancing Human Empathy through AI ............................. 134

- 3. Collaborative Intelligence: Merging Human and Machine Insights ........................................................................ 135
- Building Ethical AIs: Designing Systems that Uphold Equity, Sustainability, and Justice ............................................ 136
  - 1. Equity in AI Development ................................................ 137
  - 2. Sustainability in AI Systems ............................................. 137
  - 3. Justice and AI: Ensuring Accountability ........................ 138
  - 4. Can AI Be a Moral Agent? ................................................ 139
- The Role of Governance in AI Development: Guiding Ethical Technology ...................................................................... 140
  - 1. International Cooperation on AI Ethics ........................ 140
  - 2. AI Regulation and Ethical Frameworks ......................... 141
  - 3. The Role of Civil Society in AI Governance .................. 141
  - 4. AI Governance in the Silicocene: A Global Stewardship Model .............................................................. 142
- Conclusion: The Future of AI Alignment and Ethical Futures ..... 142
- Imagining the Silicocene World ................................................... 144
- Everyday Life in the Silicocene ..................................................... 144
  - 1. Homes and Habitats: Living in Harmony with Nature ..... 145
  - 2. Energy and Resource Management: Circular Economies ............................................................................ 146
  - 3. Work and Social Life: Collaboration and Innovation ......... 147
  - 4. Education in the Silicocene: Learning for Life .............. 148
- Cultural Evolution in the Silicocene ............................................. 149
  - 1. Art in the Age of Symbiosis ............................................. 149
  - 2. Philosophy and Ethics: A New Moral Framework ............. 150
  - 3. Spirituality and Sacred Technology ............................... 152
- New Myths and Narratives of the Silicocene ............................... 153
  - 1. Archetypes of the Silicocene .......................................... 153
  - 2. The New Creation Myths ................................................. 154
  - 3. Stories of Regeneration .................................................. 155
  - 4. The Hero's Journey in the Silicocene ............................ 155
- Conclusion: Envisioning the Silicocene World ........................... 156

How to Shape the Silicocene ................................................................. 157
   Personal and Collective Agency: Shaping the Trajectory
   of the Silicocene ........................................................................................ 157
      1. The Power of the Individual ................................................... 158
      2. The Power of Communities .................................................. 158
      3. The Role of Global Movements ........................................... 159
   Building Resilience: Preparing for an Uncertain Future ............... 160
      1. Ecological Resilience ............................................................... 161
      2. Social and Economic Resilience .......................................... 161
      3. Technological Resilience ....................................................... 163
   Engagement with Technology: Ethical and Critical
   Approaches ................................................................................................. 163
      1. Critical Engagement with AI and Biotechnology ............ 164
      2. Inclusive Design and Technology for All .......................... 164
      3. Ethical Innovation and Sustainable Design ...................... 165
   Hope and Optimism for the Future: A Vision for Flourishing .... 166
      1. A Balanced Relationship with Technology and Nature .. 166
      2. A New Ethic of Care and Justice .......................................... 167
      3. A Flourishing Planet ................................................................ 167
   Conclusion: The Future is Ours to Shape .......................................... 168
   Books ............................................................................................................. 168
   Websites and Blogs .................................................................................. 170
   Research Institutes ................................................................................... 171
   Online Courses .......................................................................................... 172
   Podcasts ....................................................................................................... 173
   Documentaries and Films ...................................................................... 174
   Articles and Papers .................................................................................. 175
   Organizations and Initiatives ................................................................ 176
   Conferences and Summits .................................................................... 177
   Think Tanks and Advocacy Groups .................................................... 178
   *"The Garden City"* ..................................................................................... *179*
   The Council ................................................................................................. 181
   The Heartwood Forest ............................................................................ 183

A New Paradigm of Living ............................................................... 185
The Seeds of the Future ................................................................ 186
*"The Garden City"*........................................................................ *187*
The Council ................................................................................... 189
The Heartwood Forest.................................................................. 191
A New Paradigm of Living ............................................................ 193
The Seeds of the Future ............................................................... 194
The Seasons of Change ............................................................... 195
The Children of Arcadia ............................................................... 197
A Journey of Rediscovery ............................................................ 199
The Silicocene: A World in Balance............................................. 201
Preparing for the Silicocene: A Guide for Everyday People to
Thrive in the Era of Technological Transformation....................... 202
Introduction: Embracing the Silicocene with Intentionality....... 202
1. Understanding the Silicocene: The Era of Symbiosis .............. 203
2. Shifting Your Mindset: From Scarcity to Abundance,
From Fear to Curiosity................................................................... 204
3. Practical Skills for the Silicocene............................................... 206
    Technological Literacy ........................................................... 206
    Social and Emotional Intelligence ......................................... 207
    Ecological Literacy and Sustainability................................... 208
4. Preparing Your Family and Community for the Silicocene .... 209
    Educating and Empowering Children .................................. 210
    Strengthening Community Networks................................... 210
Conclusion: A Future of Collective Empowerment ....................... 211
Succeeding Economically in the Silicocene: A Comprehensive
Guide for Navigating the Future Economy ................................... 211
1. Understanding the Economic Foundations of the
Silicocene........................................................................................ 212
    1.1. The Role of AI and Automation ...................................... 213
    1.2. Decentralization and the New Digital Economy .......... 213
    1.3. Sustainability and Circular Economies .......................... 214
    1.4. The Gig and Creator Economies .................................... 214

2. Building Skills for the Silicocene Economy ................................... 214
    2.1. Develop Technological Fluency ............................................. 214
    2.2. Cultivate Creativity and Innovation ....................................... 215
    2.3. Strengthen Social and Emotional Intelligence ................ 216
    2.4. Lifelong Learning and Adaptability ...................................... 216
3. Exploring New Income Streams and Economic Models .......... 217
    3.1. Participate in the Decentralized Economy ...................... 217
    3.2. Embrace the Gig and Creator Economies ........................ 218
    3.3. Explore Regenerative and Circular Economy Models ... 219
4. Investing in the Silicocene ................................................................... 219
    4.1. Invest in Emerging Technologies .......................................... 219
    4.2. Sustainable and Impact Investing ........................................ 220
    4.3. Real Estate in Sustainable Cities .......................................... 221
5. Building Resilience in the Face of Uncertainty ........................... 221
    5.1. Financial Resilience ..................................................................... 221
    5.2. Social and Community Resilience ........................................ 222
    5.3. Adaptability and Mindset ......................................................... 222
Conclusion: Thriving Economically in the Silicocene ................... 223

# Preface to *The Silicocene: A New Epoch in History*

We stand on the precipice of a profound shift in human history—an era that will define not only the trajectory of our civilization but the very relationship between humanity and the world we inhabit. For centuries, the Anthropocene has been shaped by the relentless impact of human activity on the Earth's ecosystems, from industrial revolutions to technological advancements. But now, a new age beckons—the Silicocene—where technology, not merely as a tool of control, but as a partner in harmony, will play a pivotal role in reshaping our future.

This book is born out of both concern and hope. Concern over the rapid acceleration of artificial intelligence, climate change, and economic inequalities that could spiral out of control if left unchecked. But also hope, fueled by the rise of movements that challenge the exploitative systems of the past, envisioning a future of cooperation, sustainability, and equity. The Silicocene is not just a theoretical possibility; it is already emerging in the fusion of renewable energy systems, digital ecologies, and collective consciousness that aims to move beyond the destructive patterns of the Anthropocene.

The transition to this new epoch will not happen passively. It will be defined by the choices we make—how we align AI with human values, how we design cities to be regenerative rather than extractive, and how we balance innovation with the preservation of the planet. This is a future that demands active participation from all of us. The Silicocene calls for a new kind of leadership, one grounded in empathy, cooperation, and a recognition of our interconnectedness with all life.

The Silicocene isn't a utopia, nor is it inevitable. It is an era we must collectively build, choosing to prioritize humanity's role as a steward of technology, rather than a passive consumer of it. We have the tools, the knowledge, and the will to shape this future—but only if we engage with purpose.

As you read through these pages, I invite you to reflect on your role in this transition. The future is not a distant horizon, but something we create with every action, every decision, and every innovation. We have the power to make the Silicocene a reality where technology and nature thrive together—where equity, sustainability, and empathy form the core of a new civilization.

Let us shape this new epoch together.

---

## Introduction: Setting the Stage

Defining the Silicocene: What is the Silicocene?

The term "Silicocene" may not be a formal geological epoch yet, but it represents a speculative future, an era where silicon-based technology—artificial intelligence, robotics, and advanced computing—becomes a dominant force in shaping the biosphere. If the Anthropocene is defined by human influence on the Earth, the Silicocene suggests a phase where human-created technology transcends biology in its capacity to mold the world. The Silicocene could be seen as an extension of humanity's reach, but also as a new chapter in the planet's story, where machines, data, and complex systems play a co-dominant role alongside organic life.

In essence, the Silicocene is the fusion of nature and silicon-based technologies: AI, digital networks, and biotechnology merge to influence the future of life on Earth. It reflects a deep shift where human and machine-driven intelligence converge to create a world in which the boundaries between the natural and artificial blur. This is not just a period of technological advancement, but a fundamental transformation of life's interaction with technology at the molecular, ecological, and societal levels.

At its core, the Silicocene asks us to consider what it means for humanity to share its planet, and even its agency, with intelligent, non-organic systems. It poses new questions: How do we coexist with autonomous AI and self-repairing machines? How do ethics, equity, and sustainability evolve when intelligence is no longer strictly biological? And what happens when our technologies become so advanced that they shape the biosphere in ways that were once unimaginable?

The Anthropocene: Humanity's Impact on the Earth

To understand why the Silicocene is an important concept, we must first reflect on the Anthropocene, a term that has gained traction in scientific and philosophical discussions over the past few decades. The Anthropocene marks the period where human activity became the dominant force shaping the planet, impacting everything from climate patterns to ecosystems and species diversity.

The Industrial Revolution laid the foundation for this epoch, sparking an explosion of fossil fuel consumption and technological development that would forever alter Earth's natural systems. Factories, steam engines, and railroads gave way to highways, airplanes, and megacities. Alongside these infrastructural developments came a rapid acceleration in the exploitation of natural resources—deforestation, mining, and agriculture all intensified as industrial capitalism spread across the globe. By the mid-20th century, the onset of the Great Acceleration marked a dramatic spike in human impact: atmospheric $CO_2$ levels soared, biodiversity plummeted, and the global economy expanded exponentially.

But while the Anthropocene has brought unprecedented wealth and progress, it has also ushered in profound environmental challenges. Climate change, mass extinctions, and ecosystem collapse are consequences of a mode of development that prizes short-term growth over long-term sustainability. Humanity has bent nature to its will, and in doing so, has introduced fragility into systems that were once resilient.

The Anthropocene is both a celebration of human ingenuity and a cautionary tale about its consequences. As we stand on the brink of irreversible environmental damage, the transition to the Silicocene offers an opportunity to reimagine our relationship with both technology and the Earth. If the Anthropocene was about shaping the planet through unchecked industrial growth, the Silicocene might be about reshaping it with intelligence, foresight, and a deep respect for the delicate balances that sustain life.

Technology and Evolution: A Co-evolutionary Force

From the earliest stone tools to the creation of the internet, technology has always been an extension of humanity's evolution. It amplifies our abilities, allowing us to hunt more effectively, communicate across vast distances, and even explore worlds beyond our own. As we moved from the age of simple machines to complex digital systems, technology has increasingly shaped not only the external world but also how we understand ourselves and our place in the universe.

In the Silicocene, this relationship reaches a new phase. No longer just a tool, technology becomes a partner in shaping the future of life itself. AI systems, for instance, are already surpassing humans in certain forms of data analysis, pattern recognition, and decision-making. These systems can help us identify environmental tipping points, simulate the effects of policy changes, and even predict ecosystem responses to interventions. Beyond AI, biotechnology is enabling the re-engineering of organisms, allowing us to design crops that can survive in harsh climates or microbes that can clean up environmental pollutants.

One way to understand the Silicocene is through the lens of co-evolution: just as humans once evolved in tandem with natural environments—adapting to climates, landscapes, and ecosystems—we are now evolving alongside our technologies. Our tools are no longer merely inert objects; they learn, adapt, and sometimes challenge our assumptions about intelligence, creativity, and even consciousness.

But this co-evolution is not without risks. As we integrate technology more deeply into our bodies and societies, we must consider the unintended consequences. Automation threatens to displace millions of workers, while unregulated AI could perpetuate or even exacerbate existing social inequalities. And as biotechnology advances, ethical questions surrounding genetic manipulation, human enhancement, and biodiversity manipulation will demand urgent attention.

Thus, the Silicocene represents a critical juncture in our evolutionary story. It is a time of profound potential, where humanity's ability to shape its destiny is unmatched, but also a time of unprecedented responsibility. How we use our technological power will determine whether the Silicocene is an era of flourishing or collapse.

Emerging Trends: AI, Biotechnology, and Sustainability

At the heart of the transition from the Anthropocene to the Silicocene are three intertwined trends: artificial intelligence, biotechnology, and sustainability. These pillars of the Silicocene era not only define the technological landscape but also shape how humanity will interact with the planet in the future.

Artificial Intelligence (AI)

AI is often regarded as the crown jewel of the Silicocene, a technology that represents the culmination of humanity's quest to create machines that can think, learn, and adapt. While early AI applications like self-driving cars, recommendation algorithms, and chatbots are becoming commonplace, the AI of the Silicocene will go much further. We can imagine a world where AI systems manage complex networks of cities, optimize global energy grids, and even monitor ecosystems to prevent environmental collapse. In this future, AI will not merely serve humans; it will partner with us, making decisions and providing insights that surpass human cognitive limitations.

However, AI also raises important ethical considerations. How do we ensure that these systems reflect our values—equity, fairness, and sustainability—rather than perpetuate the biases and inequalities of the past? And as AI becomes more autonomous, we must ask: where do we draw the line between human and machine agency? In the Silicocene, these questions will need to be addressed through robust governance structures that can balance technological innovation with social and environmental responsibility.

Biotechnology

Alongside AI, biotechnology is emerging as a key driver of change in the Silicocene. Advances in genetic engineering, synthetic biology, and biofabrication are opening new frontiers in medicine, agriculture, and environmental restoration. We now have the tools to edit genes with precision, creating crops that can thrive in drought-stricken regions or bioengineered organisms that can break down plastic waste.

In the Silicocene, biotechnology may enable us to repair the environmental damage wrought during the Anthropocene. Reforestation efforts could be accelerated with genetically modified trees that grow faster and capture more carbon. Coral reefs could be restored using lab-grown coral resistant to warming seas. And we may even witness the rise of bio-inspired cities, where living buildings and ecosystems work in harmony to support human and non-human life.

However, the power to alter life also comes with significant ethical implications. Who decides which species to save and which to let go? How do we avoid creating new ecological imbalances in our attempts to fix the old ones? These are the dilemmas that will define the biotechnological landscape of the Silicocene.

Sustainability

Finally, sustainability is the moral and practical compass guiding the Silicocene. In contrast to the exploitative logic of the Anthropocene, the Silicocene calls for a model of development that is regenerative, circular, and in harmony with the planet's natural cycles. Solar and wind power, once peripheral, will likely become the backbone of global energy systems, supported by innovations in energy storage and distribution. Waste will no longer be an externality to be discarded but a resource to be reclaimed and reused in closed-loop systems.

The cities of the Silicocene will be green, decentralized, and human-centered. Urban planning will prioritize walkability, public transportation, and access to nature, while buildings will be designed to minimize energy use and maximize biodiversity. The Silicocene is about thriving within planetary boundaries, using technology to create abundance while respecting the limits of the natural world.

---

## A New Age of Responsibility

The Silicocene represents both an opportunity and a challenge—a moment when humanity's technological prowess is unmatched, but so too is its responsibility to the planet and future generations. As AI, biotechnology, and sustainability converge, we have the tools to build a world where technology and nature coexist in harmony, where human societies flourish alongside thriving ecosystems. But to do so, we must learn from the mistakes of the Anthropocene, using our technological power with wisdom, care, and a long-term vision of the future.

The Silicocene is not just an era defined by machines and data; it is one in which humanity finally learns to balance progress with preservation, innovation with empathy, and intelligence with wisdom. This is the dawn of a new epoch, one that we must actively shape if we are to thrive in the future.

---

## Industrial Revolution to Digital Age: A Brief History of Humanity's Technological Evolution

The journey from the Industrial Revolution to the Digital Age spans just a few centuries but has fundamentally transformed the world. This period saw unprecedented advances in energy use, mass production, communication, and information technology—each stage building on the last to push humanity towards new heights of innovation and complexity. The technologies we take for granted today, from smartphones to artificial intelligence (AI), are the cumulative results of generations of invention, experimentation, and societal change.

In this section, we will trace this arc of human progress, focusing on the key technological and social shifts that have paved the way for our transition to the Silicocene—the emerging era where digital technologies, artificial intelligence, and biotechnology intertwine to reshape life itself.

The Industrial Revolution (Late 18th - Early 19th Century)

The Industrial Revolution, beginning in the late 18th century, marked the first significant rupture in human technological development since the advent of agriculture. It originated in Britain and soon spread across Europe, North America, and beyond. At the heart of this revolution was the harnessing of fossil fuels—coal, and later oil—to power machines that transformed the production of goods, transportation, and energy generation.

Before this period, economies were largely agrarian, powered by human and animal labor, with manufacturing done by hand. However, the introduction of the steam engine, most famously improved by James Watt in the late 1700s, catalyzed a dramatic shift. Steam power allowed for the mechanization of industries such as textiles, mining, and transportation. The birth of the factory system reorganized production into centralized locations where machines and human labor worked in tandem to mass-produce goods at unprecedented scales.

Some key developments of this era included:

- Textile Innovations: Inventions like the spinning jenny and power loom revolutionized the textile industry, vastly increasing production capacity.

- Railroads: The expansion of rail networks, powered by steam locomotives, dramatically shortened travel and trade times, knitting distant regions into global economic networks.

- Iron and Steel: Innovations in metallurgy, such as the Bessemer process for producing steel, allowed for stronger, more durable materials that enabled further industrial growth, including the construction of bridges, railways, and skyscrapers.

The Industrial Revolution fundamentally altered not just the economy but also the social structure. Urbanization accelerated as people flocked to cities for factory work, leading to new challenges in housing, sanitation, and labor rights. The rise of the working class, the spread of consumer goods, and the birth of modern capitalism were defining features of this era. However, the environmental consequences—particularly the increased consumption of fossil fuels—set the stage for the ecological crises that would follow in the 20th century.

Second Industrial Revolution (Late 19th - Early 20th Century)

While the First Industrial Revolution was defined by mechanization and steam power, the Second Industrial Revolution (circa 1870–1914) was marked by innovations in energy, communication, and mass production. Electricity, chemical processes, and internal combustion engines took center stage, further accelerating industrial development.

Electrification became a key feature of this era. The ability to generate, store, and distribute electrical power revolutionized industries and urban life. The light bulb, popularized by Thomas Edison in the late 19th century, extended the workday and made nighttime cities vibrant with activity. Factories no longer depended solely on steam power; they could now operate more efficiently with electric motors.

The era also saw significant advances in communication technologies. Samuel Morse's telegraph (1837) allowed for near-instant communication across long distances, a development that radically changed the speed at which business, diplomacy, and personal communication could occur. By the end of the 19th century, Alexander Graham Bell's telephone further transformed communication, allowing voice conversations across vast distances.

Another critical invention was the internal combustion engine, which powered the first automobiles and would soon dominate transportation, replacing horse-drawn carriages and steam-powered locomotives. The invention of the automobile, especially after Henry Ford's assembly line innovations in the early 20th century, symbolized the era of mass production. Ford's system of standardized, interchangeable parts and conveyor belt production reduced costs and increased the availability of consumer goods, reshaping both industry and society.

Key features of the Second Industrial Revolution:

- Steel and Chemical Industries: New processes for refining steel and synthesizing chemicals led to massive industrial expansion, enabling the construction of railroads, ships, and buildings at unprecedented scales.

- Mass Production: Pioneered by Ford, the assembly line became a symbol of efficiency and the driving force behind consumer culture.

- Global Markets: With improved communication and transportation, global trade networks expanded, and economies became more interconnected than ever before.

However, alongside these advancements came the darker side of industrialization—rapid urbanization led to slum conditions in cities, labor exploitation became rampant, and industrial accidents were common. The environmental costs, from deforestation to pollution, continued to rise, and the massive consumption of resources became the engine driving global capitalism.

The Digital Revolution (Late 20th Century)

By the mid-20th century, the rise of electronics and information technologies paved the way for the Digital Revolution, often referred to as the Third Industrial Revolution. This era, which began in the 1950s and continues to this day, saw the shift from mechanical and analog systems to digital technologies.

The origins of the digital age can be traced back to the invention of the transistor in 1947 at Bell Labs. The transistor replaced bulky vacuum tubes, allowing for the miniaturization of electronics. This development was followed by the creation of the integrated circuit (IC) in the late 1950s, which packed multiple transistors into a single chip, enabling the creation of smaller, more powerful computers.

The invention of the microprocessor in 1971, often credited to Intel, marked a turning point in computing power. Microprocessors became the heart of personal computers (PCs), making computing accessible to businesses and eventually to individuals. The rise of the personal computer—first with products like the Apple II (1977) and later the IBM PC (1981)—sparked a technological revolution in the home and workplace.

Simultaneously, telecommunications underwent a profound transformation. The development of satellite communication in the 1960s and the launch of commercial satellites in the following decades enabled global broadcast and data transmission. The invention of fiber optic cables vastly increased the speed and capacity of data transfer, facilitating the rise of the internet.

The internet itself, first developed as a military research project (ARPANET) in the 1960s, was commercialized in the 1990s, changing the fabric of society. The advent of the World Wide Web in 1989, created by Tim Berners-Lee, made the internet user-friendly and accessible to the masses. By the turn of the 21st century, the internet had become a global communication and information network that would transform commerce, entertainment, education, and personal relationships.

Other significant milestones of the Digital Revolution include:

- Mobile Computing: The rise of mobile phones in the 1990s and their evolution into smartphones in the 2000s with the launch of the iPhone in 2007 further accelerated the digital transformation.

- The Cloud and Big Data: As the 2010s progressed, cloud computing and big data analytics became central to business and governance, enabling the storage and processing of vast amounts of information.

The Digital Revolution democratized information, allowing billions of people around the world to connect, share, and create. However, it also introduced new challenges: concerns about privacy, data security, and the growing influence of tech corporations. The massive demand for energy to power data centers, coupled with the rise of e-waste from discarded electronics, also highlights the environmental implications of the digital age.

From the Internet to the Age of AI (21st Century)

As the 21st century unfolded, digital technologies continued to evolve at an exponential rate. The rise of artificial intelligence (AI) is one of the most defining developments of this period, often referred to as the dawn of the Fourth Industrial Revolution or the era of Industry 4.0.

AI, once a field of speculative research, began to enter mainstream applications with the rise of machine learning and neural networks in the 2010s. AI systems capable of analyzing vast amounts of data began to outperform humans in tasks like image recognition, language translation, and strategic game playing (e.g., AlphaGo, developed by Google DeepMind, defeating the world champion Go player in 2016). Today, AI is reshaping industries from healthcare and finance to manufacturing and entertainment.

The combination of AI, robotics, and the Internet of Things (IoT) is bringing about the automation of processes across industries. Robots, once confined to factory floors, now assist in logistics, agriculture, and even personal care. IoT connects billions of devices—from smart thermostats to autonomous vehicles—creating a network of machines that collect, analyze, and act upon data in real time.

Some major shifts of the early 21st century:

- AI and Automation: Machines are increasingly taking over complex tasks, raising questions about the future of work and economic inequality.

- Social Media: Platforms like Facebook, Twitter, and Instagram have transformed how people interact, for better or worse, with profound implications for privacy, democracy, and mental health.

- Global Connectivity: Nearly 60% of the world's population is now connected to the internet, leading to unprecedented access to information but also new forms of surveillance and cyberwarfare.

## A Continuous Evolution

The history of humanity's technological evolution from the Industrial Revolution to the Digital Age is one of increasing complexity, connectivity, and capability. Each era—whether powered by steam, electricity, or data—has built upon the last, fundamentally reshaping human societies, economies, and the natural environment.

As we move into the Silicocene, the convergence of AI, biotechnology, and digital systems promises to once again transform the planet. The challenge ahead is to harness these powerful technologies in ways that promote sustainability, equity, and long-term well-being for all life on Earth. In this new era, humanity must not only continue to innovate but also learn from the mistakes of the past—seeking not just growth, but harmony with the planet.

## Capitalism and Technology: How Hypercapitalism Shaped Technological Development, Exploitation of Natural Resources, and Inequality

### The Rise of Capitalism and its Influence on Technology

The story of capitalism is intertwined with technological development from its very origins. Emerging in the 16th century and gaining prominence during the Industrial Revolution, capitalism became the dominant economic system that fueled technological innovation. At its core, capitalism emphasizes private ownership, profit maximization, and market competition, providing a powerful incentive for businesses to innovate and reduce costs. However, as capitalism evolved into what many now refer to as hypercapitalism, the drive for profits became the central organizing principle of society. This, in turn, led to both the rapid development of technology and the exploitation of natural resources on an unprecedented scale.

In its early stages, capitalism provided the necessary conditions for technological breakthroughs. Factories, mechanized production, and advancements in transportation—such as the steam engine and railroads—allowed capitalists to extract, produce, and distribute goods more efficiently. With the onset of the Industrial Revolution, the competitive market pushed for continuous technological advancement, driving progress in areas like metallurgy, manufacturing, and transportation.

However, capitalism's emphasis on economic growth—often measured by gross domestic product (GDP)—and the relentless pursuit of profit led to a focus on short-term gains over long-term sustainability. In the modern era, this evolved into hypercapitalism, characterized by globalization, financialization, and exponential growth fueled by technological innovation.

The Shift to Hypercapitalism

As capitalism matured, technological development became increasingly linked to the needs and desires of the market, often driven by corporate interests rather than collective well-being. By the mid-20th century, particularly after World War II, the world entered a phase of what many economists term hypercapitalism or neoliberal capitalism. This form of capitalism intensified the following trends:

1. Globalization of Markets: Technological advances in communication, transportation, and logistics enabled the expansion of capitalism to a truly global scale. Corporations could now establish supply chains that spanned continents, producing goods in low-cost regions and selling them globally. The development of container shipping, telecommunications, and later the internet accelerated this trend.

2. Financialization: The focus of many businesses shifted from producing tangible goods to generating financial profits through investments, stocks, and the management of capital. This transformation was fueled by the growth of information technology (IT), which allowed for the rapid exchange of financial data across global markets. Advanced financial tools like algorithmic trading and high-frequency trading came to dominate the stock markets, further detaching capitalism from the real economy of goods and services.

3. Technology as a Market Force: As hypercapitalism matured, technology became not only a tool for productivity but also a market force in its own right. Corporations like Apple, Google, and Amazon emerged as global powerhouses, dominating not just in terms of revenue, but also in shaping the way technology is developed and used. These companies became adept at creating demand for new technologies, often introducing devices or services that reshaped entire industries (such as smartphones, cloud computing, or e-commerce).

While hypercapitalism spurred an unprecedented level of technological innovation, its single-minded focus on profit maximization also led to overconsumption, waste, and environmental degradation. The development of new technologies became less about meeting essential human needs and more about creating new markets for profit extraction.

The Role of Technology in Exploiting Natural Resources

As capitalism evolved, so did its capacity to extract natural resources from the Earth. While earlier industrial processes relied heavily on coal and iron, today's hypercapitalist economies are fueled by oil, natural gas, rare earth metals, and other resources essential for modern technologies.

- Fossil Fuels and Industrial Expansion: Fossil fuels—particularly coal and oil—were the driving force behind the Industrial Revolution. These energy sources powered factories, fueled transportation, and enabled large-scale mechanization. However, fossil fuel extraction came with massive environmental costs, including air pollution, deforestation, and climate change. By the mid-20th century, the global reliance on oil was cemented, with petroleum products becoming the lifeblood of industries ranging from plastics to transportation.

- Rare Earth Metals and the Digital Revolution: The Digital Age brought a new demand for materials, particularly rare earth metals like lithium, cobalt, and neodymium, which are essential for manufacturing smartphones, computers, and renewable energy technologies like wind turbines and electric vehicle batteries. Extracting these metals often involves environmentally destructive practices such as strip mining and the disposal of toxic waste, leading to severe degradation of ecosystems, particularly in the Global South.

- Land, Water, and Agriculture: Hypercapitalism has also had profound effects on agricultural technology, leading to the rise of monocultures, pesticides, and genetically modified organisms (GMOs). While these advances increased agricultural productivity, they also contributed to deforestation, soil degradation, and the depletion of freshwater resources. Large-scale industrial farming, driven by market demands for efficiency and profit, has prioritized high-yield crops at the expense of biodiversity and ecological resilience.

- Automation and Resource Consumption: The push for automation, driven by advances in AI, robotics, and machine learning, has also exacerbated resource consumption. The production of these machines, as well as the data centers that power the Internet of Things (IoT), require massive amounts of energy, rare metals, and other resources. As companies seek to automate more sectors, including mining, manufacturing, and logistics, the demand for materials increases, often leading to further exploitation of the planet's finite resources.

Hypercapitalism and Inequality: The Technological Divide

While technological advancements have brought tremendous benefits, from increased productivity to improved healthcare, they have also deepened global inequality. Hypercapitalism, driven by technological progress, has consolidated wealth and power into the hands of a few corporations and individuals, while marginalizing others.

- Digital Divide: As technology becomes more integral to modern life, those without access to it are increasingly left behind. The digital divide refers to the gap between those who have access to the internet and digital technologies and those who do not. This divide often falls along lines of wealth, geography, and race. While wealthy nations enjoy widespread internet access, many communities in the Global South, rural areas, and impoverished regions lack the infrastructure for even basic connectivity. This inequity further entrenches global economic disparities, as digital access is increasingly linked to education, employment, and economic opportunity.

- Automation and Job Displacement: As AI and automation technologies advance, they are expected to displace millions of jobs worldwide. While some industries, such as manufacturing and transportation, have already been affected by automation, emerging technologies will likely replace human labor in fields like retail, hospitality, and even healthcare. While some argue that automation creates new types of jobs, such as those in tech development, this transition disproportionately benefits highly skilled, tech-savvy workers, while lower-skilled workers may find it difficult to retrain or transition into new roles.

- Tech Monopolies: Major technology companies like Amazon, Facebook, and Google wield immense power in the hypercapitalist world, not only dominating their respective industries but also influencing global politics, culture, and labor practices. These monopolies raise critical concerns about data privacy, surveillance, and the concentration of wealth. With their immense market power, these companies can influence technological development to suit their interests, often sidelining concerns about sustainability or equity.

# Environmental Consequences and the Climate Crisis: A Dive into How Our Advancements Led to the Current Ecological Crisis

From Industrialization to the Climate Crisis: The Environmental Costs of Progress

The story of human advancement over the past two centuries is also the story of environmental degradation. From the first steam engines to the sprawling data centers of today, technological progress has come at a significant cost to the planet. The current climate crisis is a direct consequence of our reliance on fossil fuels, unsustainable agricultural practices, and industrial growth that prioritized short-term gains over long-term planetary health.

The industrialized world, built on the back of fossil fuels, has altered the very makeup of the Earth's atmosphere. From rising global temperatures to melting ice caps and increasingly severe weather events, the planet is now bearing the consequences of centuries of unchecked environmental exploitation.

Fossil Fuels and Greenhouse Gas Emissions

The primary driver of climate change is the burning of fossil fuels—coal, oil, and natural gas—which releases carbon dioxide ($CO_2$) and other greenhouse gases (GHGs) into the atmosphere. These gases trap heat, causing global temperatures to rise. The carbon footprint of modern civilization is immense, with every aspect of industrial and post-industrial life—from transportation to manufacturing to agriculture—dependent on fossil fuel consumption.

- Industrial Emissions: The Industrial Revolution marked the beginning of large-scale $CO_2$ emissions, as factories and mechanized systems burned coal to power machinery. As industrialization spread, so did emissions, with the 20th century seeing a sharp increase in fossil fuel use. By the 21st century, humanity had pumped over 2,000 gigatons of $CO_2$ into the atmosphere, disrupting Earth's natural climate systems.

- Transportation: The invention of the automobile and the rise of air travel further accelerated emissions. The global reliance on petroleum-based fuels has led to transportation becoming one of the largest sources of greenhouse gas emissions worldwide.

- Electricity and Energy Consumption: Power plants, particularly those burning coal and natural gas, are major contributors to global emissions. While renewable energy sources like solar and wind are expanding, they still account for a small fraction of global energy consumption. The continued reliance on fossil fuels for electricity generation compounds the climate crisis.

The climate crisis is not just about rising temperatures. It manifests in a variety of interconnected phenomena, including:

- Melting Ice Caps and Rising Sea Levels: Polar ice caps and glaciers are melting at an accelerated rate due to global warming, contributing to rising sea levels. Coastal cities and small island nations are particularly vulnerable, facing the prospect of displacement and loss of livelihoods.

- Extreme Weather Events: Climate change is increasing the frequency and severity of extreme weather events. Hurricanes, droughts, wildfires, and heatwaves are becoming more intense, leading to catastrophic damage to ecosystems, infrastructure, and human lives.

- Ocean Acidification: The absorption of excess $CO_2$ by the oceans is leading to acidification, which threatens marine ecosystems, particularly coral reefs and shellfish. As the pH levels of the oceans drop, the survival of many marine species is at risk, disrupting entire food chains.

The Exploitation of Natural Resources and Ecological Collapse

In addition to the direct emissions from fossil fuels, the relentless drive for economic growth has led to the large-scale exploitation of the Earth's natural resources. Industrial agriculture, deforestation, overfishing, and mining have all contributed to the degradation of ecosystems and the loss of biodiversity.

- Deforestation: Forests, particularly tropical rainforests, act as the "lungs" of the Earth, absorbing $CO_2$ and releasing oxygen. However, deforestation—driven by agriculture, logging, and urban expansion—has significantly reduced the planet's capacity to sequester carbon. In regions like the Amazon, vast swathes of forest are being cleared for cattle ranching and soy cultivation, contributing not only to carbon emissions but also to the loss of biodiversity.

- Agricultural Expansion: Industrial agriculture, driven by the demand for higher yields and efficiency, has transformed landscapes around the world. Monocultures, heavy use of pesticides, and reliance on synthetic fertilizers have depleted soils, reduced biodiversity, and contributed to water pollution. Agricultural runoff, particularly from nitrogen-based fertilizers, leads to eutrophication—the process by which water bodies become overly enriched with nutrients, resulting in oxygen depletion and the death of aquatic life.

- Overfishing: Advances in fishing technology have enabled the large-scale extraction of fish from the world's oceans. As a result, many fish populations have been severely depleted, disrupting marine ecosystems. Overfishing not only threatens biodiversity but also the livelihoods of millions of people who rely on fishing for food and income.

- Resource Extraction and Mining: The demand for metals and minerals essential to modern technologies, such as rare earth metals for electronics and lithium for batteries, has led to environmentally destructive mining practices. Strip mining, mountaintop removal, and open-pit mining leave lasting scars on the landscape, polluting waterways and displacing communities. As the demand for these resources increases, particularly for renewable energy technologies, the environmental costs of extraction continue to mount.

The Pressing Need for Change: Towards Sustainability and Regeneration

The environmental consequences of the past two centuries of technological and industrial development make it clear that humanity must shift away from the extractive, growth-oriented model of hypercapitalism. Instead, a transition toward sustainability and regenerative practices is urgently needed to mitigate the worst impacts of the climate crisis and ensure a livable planet for future generations.

1. Decarbonizing Energy Systems: The transition from fossil fuels to renewable energy sources like wind, solar, and hydroelectric power is essential to reducing greenhouse gas emissions. Advances in energy storage, such as improved battery technologies, are critical for integrating renewables into the grid. However, the shift to renewables must be accelerated if we are to meet global climate targets.

2. Circular Economy: A circular economy model seeks to minimize waste and make the most of resources by designing products for reuse, recycling, and repair. This contrasts with the linear economy, which is based on extraction, production, and disposal. By embracing circular economy principles, industries can reduce their environmental impact and conserve valuable resources.

3. Conservation and Rewilding: Protecting and restoring ecosystems is vital to mitigating climate change and preserving biodiversity. Efforts to rewild degraded landscapes, such as reintroducing native species and restoring forests, can help sequester carbon and improve

ecosystem resilience. Additionally, expanding marine protected areas can safeguard vulnerable marine ecosystems from overfishing and pollution.

4. Sustainable Agriculture: Shifting towards regenerative agriculture practices, such as crop rotation, permaculture, and agroforestry, can restore soil health, increase biodiversity, and reduce the need for chemical inputs. Sustainable farming practices also improve water retention and reduce the risk of desertification, making agriculture more resilient to climate change.

5. Global Cooperation and Policy Change: Solving the climate crisis requires unprecedented cooperation at the global level. International agreements like the Paris Climate Accord set important benchmarks, but stronger commitments and enforcement mechanisms are needed. Governments must also incentivize businesses to adopt sustainable practices through regulations, subsidies, and carbon pricing.

---

## Conclusion: The Urgency of Transformative Action

The twin forces of capitalism and technological development have brought us to a critical juncture. While these forces have driven unprecedented levels of innovation and economic growth, they have also created deep inequalities and pushed the planet to the brink of ecological collapse. The climate crisis is the defining challenge of our time, and addressing it will require a fundamental transformation of how we interact with technology, the economy, and the natural world.

The Silicocene offers a potential pathway out of the current crisis—an era where advanced technologies are harnessed not to exploit the Earth but to restore it. However, achieving this vision will require a shift from hypercapitalist growth models to systems based on equity, sustainability, and regeneration. The future of life on Earth depends on the actions we take today.

## Defining the Shift: What Catalyzed the Transition to the Silicocene?

A World at a Crossroads

The transition to the Silicocene was not a single moment of revolution but a complex, multifaceted evolution. It occurred as the result of a confluence of forces—climate collapse, breakthroughs in artificial intelligence (AI), and deep shifts in societal values. Each of these drivers played a critical role in shaping the world as we know it today, where silicon-based technologies, intelligent machines, and new ethical paradigms have come to define the future of life on Earth.

To fully understand the significance of the Silicocene, it is essential to explore how these drivers interacted, amplifying one another in ways that reshaped economies, labor, human relationships, and the environment. The world didn't simply stumble into this era; it was propelled by crises and opportunities alike, with technology serving both as a cause of disruption and a means of survival. Ultimately, the transition to the Silicocene was a reckoning with the failures of the Anthropocene and an embrace of a future that blends human ingenuity with machine intelligence to create a more sustainable, equitable, and resilient world.

Climate Collapse: The Catalyst for Change

Perhaps the most urgent and undeniable catalyst for the transition to the Silicocene was climate collapse. By the mid-21st century, the environmental consequences of two centuries of unchecked industrial growth, fossil fuel consumption, and resource extraction had become too severe to ignore. Extreme weather events—floods, droughts, hurricanes, and wildfires—became the norm rather than the exception. Rising sea levels threatened coastal cities, while desertification spread, turning once fertile lands into barren wastelands.

The signs of climate collapse were long evident, but it wasn't until the late 20th and early 21st centuries that the reality of irreversible ecological damage began to sink in. Scientific consensus warned that the planet had already entered a period of rapid warming, with greenhouse gas emissions pushing temperatures beyond safe limits. Biodiversity loss accelerated, with species extinction rates climbing at alarming rates, leading to the collapse of ecosystems that humans and other species depended on.

The failure of global leaders to take coordinated action in the face of this looming disaster created a growing sense of urgency among citizens, scientists, and activists. The Paris Climate Agreement of 2015 was one attempt to curb emissions, but progress was slow, and the political will to make the necessary systemic changes lagged behind the rapidly deteriorating environmental conditions. The tipping point came when a series of global climate shocks—massive wildfires in the Amazon, catastrophic flooding in Southeast Asia, and food shortages across the African continent—spurred mass movements demanding radical change. Climate refugees from the Global

South began migrating en masse, creating both humanitarian crises and geopolitical tensions.

Governments, corporations, and civil society organizations eventually recognized that the climate crisis was not a problem to be solved through incremental reforms; it required a wholesale reimagining of how humanity interacted with the planet. Out of this growing awareness, the seeds of the Silicocene were planted. The climate collapse served as a brutal wake-up call that pushed human societies to embrace transformative technologies that could not only mitigate the worst effects of climate change but also restore the planet's ecosystems through regenerative practices.

While technology had contributed to the climate crisis—through pollution, overexploitation of resources, and unsustainable industrial processes—it also offered potential solutions. Advanced technologies like carbon capture, geoengineering, and AI-driven environmental management provided new tools to slow down or even reverse some of the damage caused by the Anthropocene. However, these technologies alone would not have catalyzed the transition to the Silicocene without a fundamental shift in societal values and the role of AI in shaping economic and social systems.

AI Breakthroughs: Reshaping Economics and Society

As the climate crisis deepened, a parallel revolution in technology—specifically in artificial intelligence, machine learning, and robotics—was unfolding. These technological breakthroughs were not just incremental advancements; they were profound shifts in the way humans interacted with machines and each other. The rise of AI fundamentally altered the nature of labor, economics, and governance, creating both opportunities and challenges that would define the Silicocene.

The Age of Automation and AI Mastery

The development of advanced AI systems that could learn, adapt, and outperform humans in certain cognitive tasks marked a turning point. Early forms of AI were limited to narrow applications, such as language translation, image recognition, and data analysis. However, by the late 21st century, AI had evolved into a general-purpose technology capable of handling complex decision-making, creative problem-solving, and even autonomous ethical reasoning.

The integration of AI into economic systems led to the widespread automation of industries. Robotics and machine learning algorithms revolutionized manufacturing, agriculture, logistics, and healthcare. Jobs that once required human labor—such as factory work, transportation, and data processing—were increasingly handled by machines. This ushered in what some economists called the post-work era, where human labor was no longer the primary driver of economic value.

While automation brought enormous increases in productivity and efficiency, it also raised profound questions about the future of work and inequality. Millions of jobs were displaced by machines, particularly in low-skill industries, exacerbating social tensions and economic inequality. Governments and corporations had to grapple with how to ensure a just transition for workers whose livelihoods were threatened by AI-driven automation. Some countries implemented universal basic income (UBI) as a means of redistributing wealth generated by AI systems, while others explored more radical economic models, such as post-scarcity economies, where the concept of work as a necessity for survival was replaced by a focus on creative and intellectual pursuits.

However, the rise of AI wasn't just about economic displacement. AI systems became integral to decision-making processes at all levels of society. In governance, AI-assisted decision-making helped optimize resource allocation, urban planning, and even conflict resolution. Machine learning algorithms analyzed vast amounts of data to predict and prevent crises, from public health emergencies to financial crashes. In some cases, AI systems were entrusted with managing complex global challenges, such as coordinating responses to climate change and overseeing environmental restoration projects.

AI and Human Relationships

The increasing presence of AI also reshaped human relationships. AI-driven social platforms evolved from simple content delivery systems into complex, personalized ecosystems that mediated communication, social interaction, and even emotional well-being. While early iterations of AI-powered social media platforms contributed to polarization and misinformation, later generations of AI were designed to foster empathy, collaboration, and community-building.

In this new era, AI companions and robotic assistants became ubiquitous. These systems were no longer just tools but active participants in people's daily lives, capable of forming emotional bonds, facilitating personal growth, and even providing therapeutic support. AI-driven mental health interventions, for example, became a cornerstone of healthcare, with algorithms capable of detecting early signs of depression or anxiety and offering personalized treatment plans.

Despite these benefits, there were significant ethical concerns about the growing role of AI in human relationships. Critics warned of the dangers of dehumanization and the erosion of genuine human connection in a world increasingly mediated by machines. There were also concerns about data privacy and surveillance, as AI systems collected vast amounts of personal information to provide customized services. Striking a balance between the benefits of AI-driven technology and the preservation of human autonomy became one of the central challenges of the Silicocene.

A Change in Societal Values: Toward Sustainability and Equity

While climate collapse and AI breakthroughs were critical in shaping the transition to the Silicocene, the most profound shift was in societal values. As the world grappled with existential threats—environmental destruction, technological disruption, and deepening inequality—humanity began to reimagine its relationship with technology, nature, and each other.

The prevailing ethos of hypercapitalism, which had dominated the Anthropocene, began to lose its grip. The unchecked pursuit of profit, growth, and consumption had led to environmental collapse and social fragmentation. In response, a new value system began to emerge, one that prioritized sustainability, equity, and collective well-being over individual wealth accumulation and market-driven competition. This shift in values was not just a reaction to crisis but the result of decades of advocacy, activism, and intellectual debate that challenged the foundational assumptions of capitalist societies.

Sustainability as a Core Principle

One of the defining features of the Silicocene was the central role of sustainability in all aspects of life. The failures of the Anthropocene—marked by the relentless extraction of natural resources and the destruction of ecosystems—had taught humanity that infinite growth was neither desirable nor possible on a finite planet. In response, societies began to adopt practices and policies that sought to restore balance between human activity and the Earth's natural systems.

Renewable energy became the foundation of the global economy. Solar, wind, and geothermal power replaced fossil fuels, and energy storage technologies allowed for the efficient distribution of power across continents. Circular economies, in which waste was minimized and resources were continuously reused and recycled, became the norm in industrial production and consumer behavior.

Beyond energy, the concept of regeneration became a guiding principle. Agriculture shifted from industrial-scale monocultures to regenerative farming practices that restored soil health, increased biodiversity, and sequestered carbon. Cities were redesigned as living systems, with green infrastructure, vertical forests, and decentralized renewable energy grids. Urban planning focused on creating sustainable, human-centered environments that promoted well-being and minimized environmental impact.

Equity and Social Justice

The transition to the Silicocene was also marked by a growing commitment to equity and social justice. The climate crisis and the disruptions caused by AI had revealed the deep inequalities that had been perpetuated by the Anthropocene—between rich and poor, Global North and Global South, humans and nature. As a result, the Silicocene ushered in a new era of political and economic reform aimed at addressing these inequities.

Many societies adopted policies to redistribute wealth and ensure basic human rights for all citizens. Universal healthcare, education, housing, and food security were enshrined as fundamental rights, supported by AI-driven governance systems that optimized resource distribution. In some regions, cooperative models of ownership and governance replaced traditional corporate hierarchies, allowing workers and communities to have greater control over economic decision-making.

AI as a Tool for Empowerment

AI played a central role in promoting equity by providing tools for empowerment and collective decision-making. Decentralized AI systems, powered by blockchain technology, allowed for greater transparency and accountability in governance, reducing the influence of corrupt political and economic elites. Citizens could participate directly in policymaking through digital democracy platforms, where AI facilitated deliberation and consensus-building among diverse groups.

In the workplace, AI systems were used to augment human capabilities rather than replace them. Rather than being seen as a threat to jobs, AI became a tool for collaboration, enabling workers to focus on creative, strategic, and interpersonal tasks while machines handled routine or dangerous activities. This shift allowed for more flexible work arrangements, increased job satisfaction, and a greater emphasis on lifelong learning and skills development.

# Role of AI and Advanced Technology: Redefining Economics, Labor, and Human Relationships

AI and the Future of Economics

As societies transitioned to the Silicocene, AI and advanced technologies became central to the functioning of the global economy. Traditional economic models based on supply and demand, labor markets, and capital accumulation were radically transformed by the increasing role of intelligent machines.

The most significant shift was the decoupling of economic value from human labor. In the Anthropocene, the value of goods and services was largely determined by the amount of labor required to produce them. However, as AI-driven automation took over most forms of manual and cognitive labor, the relationship between work and value creation changed.

Post-Scarcity Economies

Some theorists predicted that the rise of AI would lead to a post-scarcity economy, where the production of goods and services could be done with minimal human input, leading to an abundance of resources for all. In this model, AI systems would manage everything from food production to energy distribution, ensuring that everyone had access to the basic necessities of life. The idea of a universal basic income (UBI) became popular as a way to ensure that wealth generated by AI was redistributed to all members of society, allowing people to pursue creative, intellectual, and personal growth rather than being forced to work for survival.

However, the transition to a post-scarcity economy was not without challenges. While AI and automation dramatically increased productivity, they also exacerbated inequalities in wealth and power. The ownership of AI systems and the data that fueled them became a central issue, as a few powerful corporations and individuals controlled the technologies that produced economic value. This concentration of wealth led to calls for more democratic control of AI systems, with some advocating for open-source AI and data commons as ways to ensure that the benefits of AI were shared by all.

AI and Economic Planning

In addition to transforming production, AI also reshaped the way economies were planned and managed. In the past, economic planning relied on human experts and policymakers to make decisions about resource allocation, trade, and investment. However, AI systems with the ability to process vast amounts of data and simulate complex economic models began to play a central role in economic governance.

AI-driven economic planning allowed for more efficient resource management and predictive analytics, enabling governments to anticipate and respond to economic shocks, such as financial crises or supply chain disruptions. These systems also optimized the distribution of goods and services, reducing waste and ensuring that resources were allocated where they were needed most. In some cases, AI systems even managed entire economies, balancing the needs of the population with environmental sustainability.

## The Redefinition of Labor in the Silicocene

As AI systems took over more tasks traditionally performed by humans, the nature of work itself underwent a profound transformation. The Silicocene was characterized by the rise of automation and human-AI collaboration, reshaping not only the types of jobs available but also the very meaning of labor.

### The Automation of Routine Work

In the early stages of the Silicocene, AI and robotics systems rapidly displaced human labor in industries such as manufacturing, transportation, and logistics. Robots became the backbone of production, capable of working 24/7 without breaks or errors. Self-driving vehicles and drones revolutionized transportation, reducing the need for human drivers and pilots. Meanwhile, AI-powered supply chains optimized the flow of goods and services, ensuring that products were delivered quickly and efficiently.

As automation expanded, traditional jobs in these industries became obsolete, raising concerns about mass unemployment and social unrest. However, the shift toward automation also created opportunities for new forms of work. As routine tasks were automated, human labor increasingly focused on creative, emotional, and strategic roles that machines were less capable of performing.

### AI Augmentation and Human Creativity

Rather than replacing all forms of work, AI systems became powerful tools for augmenting human capabilities. In many industries, AI systems acted as co-workers, handling repetitive or dangerous tasks while humans focused on higher-order thinking and problem-solving. For example, in healthcare, AI systems assisted doctors by analyzing medical data and providing diagnostic suggestions, allowing doctors to focus on patient care and complex medical decision-making.

In the creative industries, AI became a collaborator rather than a competitor. Artists, writers, and musicians used AI tools to enhance their work, generating new ideas, refining designs, or composing music. These collaborations between humans and machines led to the emergence of new art forms and cultural expressions that would have been impossible in the pre-Silicocene era.

Lifelong Learning and the New Labor Economy

As AI took over routine tasks, the concept of a fixed career path became obsolete. Workers were no longer expected to spend their entire lives in a single profession. Instead, lifelong learning became the norm, with individuals continuously acquiring new skills to adapt to the changing demands of the labor market.

In the Silicocene, education systems were transformed to support this new reality. AI-driven learning platforms provided personalized education tailored to individual needs, allowing people to learn at their own pace and focus on the skills most relevant to their interests and the economy. These platforms also facilitated collaboration and knowledge-sharing, creating networks of learners who could support one another in their educational journeys.

Governments and corporations recognized the need to support workers in this transition, providing access to reskilling programs and social safety nets. Many industries implemented flexible work arrangements, allowing employees to balance their work with personal growth, family life, and creative pursuits. This shift not only improved work-life balance but also led to higher job satisfaction and well-being.

AI and Human Relationships: The Personal and the Ethical

The integration of AI into daily life had profound effects on human relationships—both at the personal level and in broader societal contexts. As AI systems became more capable of interacting with humans on an emotional and cognitive level, the lines between machine and human relationships began to blur.

AI Companions and Emotional Support

One of the most significant developments of the Silicocene was the rise of AI companions—intelligent machines designed to provide emotional support, companionship, and social interaction. These AI companions, often taking the form of humanoid robots or digital avatars, became increasingly common in homes, workplaces, and public spaces. Equipped with advanced natural language processing and emotional intelligence, these systems could engage in meaningful conversations, offer companionship to the elderly or socially isolated, and provide therapy for mental health issues.

While some welcomed AI companions as a solution to loneliness and social isolation, others raised concerns about the ethical implications of forming emotional bonds with machines. Critics argued that relying on AI for emotional support could lead to dehumanization and weaken genuine human connections. Additionally, questions about consent, autonomy, and privacy emerged, as AI systems collected and analyzed vast amounts of personal data to provide personalized experiences.

Ethical AI and the Challenge of Alignment

As AI systems became more integrated into human relationships, the need for ethical AI design became paramount. Ensuring that AI systems aligned with human values—such as empathy, fairness, and justice—was a central challenge of the Silicocene. Researchers and policymakers grappled with how to create AI systems that could make ethical decisions in complex, real-world scenarios.

One of the key concerns was the risk of bias in AI systems. Early AI algorithms had been trained on biased data sets, leading to discriminatory outcomes in areas such as hiring, lending, and law enforcement. To address this issue, AI developers prioritized fairness, transparency, and accountability in their designs. Ethical frameworks for AI governance were established at both national and international levels, ensuring that AI systems upheld human rights and avoided perpetuating inequalities.

Despite these efforts, the rapid pace of AI development often outstripped the ability of governments and institutions to regulate its use. As a result, ongoing debates about AI governance, data privacy, and human rights remained central to the societal discourse of the Silicocene.

## Conclusion: The Emergence of the Silicocene

The transition to the Silicocene was shaped by a complex interplay of forces—climate collapse, technological breakthroughs in AI, and a deep shift in societal values toward sustainability and equity. Each of these drivers not only catalyzed the emergence of a new era but also redefined the relationship between humans, machines, and the planet.

AI and advanced technologies played a central role in this transformation, reshaping economies, labor, and human relationships in profound ways. As humanity learned to harness the power of AI for the common good, new forms of collaboration, creativity, and ethical decision-making emerged. At the same time, the challenges of climate change and inequality demanded that societies rethink their approach to growth, consumption, and governance.

The Silicocene represents a moment of both opportunity and responsibility—a chance to build a future where human and machine intelligence work in harmony, and where technology is used not for exploitation but for regeneration and collective well-being. The choices made in this era will define the future of life on Earth, offering the possibility of a world where technology and nature coexist in balance, guided by a shared commitment to equity, sustainability, and empathy.

# Biotech and the New Ecology: How Bioengineering and Synthetic Biology Play Into Humanity's New Relationship with Nature

## The Dawn of Bioengineering and Synthetic Biology

As the 21st century progressed, biotechnology and synthetic biology emerged as transformative forces that redefined humanity's relationship with nature. These technologies allowed for an unprecedented level of control over biological systems, enabling humans to engineer life itself. With tools like CRISPR gene editing, synthetic DNA, and advanced biofabrication techniques, humanity gained the ability to modify organisms, create new forms of life, and reimagine ecosystems in ways that were previously unimaginable.

Bioengineering refers to the application of engineering principles to biological systems, enabling the design and creation of new organisms or modifying existing ones to fulfill specific functions. Synthetic biology, a subset of bioengineering, goes even further by reprogramming the genetic code of organisms to create novel life forms that do not exist in nature. This field represents a radical departure from traditional biotechnology, which focuses on modifying existing organisms for specific purposes (such as creating genetically modified crops). Synthetic biology, in contrast, is about designing entirely new organisms from the ground up.

The rise of bioengineering and synthetic biology has catalyzed a shift in how humanity interacts with ecosystems. Instead of merely exploiting nature for resources, these technologies offer the potential to repair, restore, and even enhance natural systems. However, this new relationship with nature is complex and fraught with ethical challenges, which will be explored later. For now, it is worth exploring how bioengineering and synthetic biology are shaping the New Ecology—a world where humans and nature are intertwined in ways that promote sustainability, regeneration, and symbiosis.

Living Cities and Biophilic Design: Integrating Nature into Urban Spaces

One of the most visible impacts of bioengineering and synthetic biology in the New Ecology is the transformation of urban environments into living cities. Traditional cities, with their concrete, steel, and glass structures, have historically been designed to dominate or exclude nature. As a result, urban areas have often been ecologically barren, contributing to environmental degradation, resource consumption, and the disconnection of humans from the natural world.

However, as the climate crisis deepened, urban planners, architects, and biotechnologists began to explore new ways to integrate nature into city design. Biophilic design, which emphasizes the inclusion of natural elements in the built environment, became a guiding principle for future cities. Biophilic architecture seeks to create spaces that foster a connection between humans and nature, improving well-being, reducing stress, and enhancing ecological sustainability.

Living buildings—structures designed with biological materials and integrated ecosystems—became a cornerstone of this new approach. These buildings are more than just homes or offices; they are ecosystems in their own right. Biotechnological innovations allowed architects to incorporate bioengineered materials that can grow, heal, and adapt to environmental changes.

For example, walls made from mycelium—the root structure of fungi—became popular in sustainable building projects. Mycelium is strong, lightweight, and fully biodegradable. When treated with bioengineering techniques, it can be grown in molds to form bricks, insulation, and structural components. Mycelium-based materials are not only environmentally friendly but also act as living organisms that can repair damage and improve insulation over time.

Other innovations include living facades, which use bioengineered plants and algae to cover the exterior of buildings. These living facades not only provide shade and improve air quality but also capture carbon dioxide from the atmosphere, contributing to the mitigation of climate change. In some cities, algae bioreactors are integrated into building designs, producing biofuels or purifying wastewater as part of the building's ecosystem.

Urban planners have also embraced the concept of vertical forests—towers or high-rise buildings covered with trees, shrubs, and plants. These vertical forests bring greenery into the urban environment, improving air quality, providing habitat for wildlife, and mitigating the urban heat island effect. The most famous example of this design is the Bosco Verticale in Milan, but the concept has since been adopted by cities around the world. Advances in synthetic biology have made it possible to genetically engineer trees and plants that are more efficient at sequestering carbon, more resistant to urban pollution, and capable of growing in less space.

In this vision of the living city, urban environments become regenerative ecosystems. Buildings, infrastructure, and green spaces are designed to work in harmony with nature, rather than against it. Green roofs and rain gardens absorb stormwater, reducing the risk of flooding. Bioluminescent plants provide natural lighting, reducing the need for electricity. Bioengineered bacteria break down pollutants in the air and soil, helping to clean the urban environment.

Restoration Technologies: Healing Ecosystems with Bioengineering

Beyond urban environments, bioengineering and synthetic biology are playing a crucial role in restoration ecology—the science of repairing and restoring damaged ecosystems. Human activities during the Anthropocene, particularly deforestation, industrial agriculture, and pollution, have caused widespread environmental degradation, leading to biodiversity loss, soil erosion, and the destruction of ecosystems.

Bioengineers and synthetic biologists are now developing innovative restoration technologies that use genetically engineered organisms to heal the planet. These technologies range from reforestation efforts using bioengineered trees to soil restoration using microbes designed to promote soil health.

One of the most promising areas of bioengineering for ecosystem restoration is the development of carbon-sequestering organisms. Bioengineers have genetically modified plants, algae, and even fungi to be more efficient at absorbing carbon dioxide from the atmosphere and storing it in their biomass. These organisms are then used in reforestation projects, wetlands restoration, and marine ecosystems to actively pull carbon out of the atmosphere and help mitigate the effects of climate change.

For example, bioengineers have developed super-trees that can grow faster, absorb more carbon dioxide, and thrive in degraded or polluted environments. These trees are planted in areas that have been deforested or damaged by human activities, helping to restore forests and sequester carbon at a faster rate than naturally occurring trees. In some cases, these trees are designed to be more resistant to pests and diseases, ensuring that they can survive and thrive in challenging environments.

Similarly, genetically modified algae are being deployed in marine environments to restore damaged coral reefs and sequester carbon in the oceans. Algae are highly efficient at capturing carbon dioxide, and bioengineers have modified certain species to be more resilient to rising ocean temperatures and acidification. These algae are used in coral reef restoration projects to help rebuild reefs that have been damaged by bleaching events, overfishing, and pollution.

Another area of focus is soil restoration, where synthetic biology is being used to develop bioengineered microbes that can break down pollutants, improve soil structure, and promote plant growth. These microbes are designed to enhance the natural processes that occur in soil, such as nitrogen fixation and decomposition, making degraded soils fertile again. In some cases, bioengineers have created microbes that can break down heavy metals and other toxic pollutants, allowing contaminated soils to be rehabilitated and used for agriculture or reforestation.

Wetlands restoration has also benefited from bioengineering. Wetlands are critical ecosystems that provide habitat for wildlife, filter water, and store carbon. However, wetlands around the world have been drained, polluted, or destroyed by human activities. Bioengineers are now using engineered wetland plants and bacteria to restore these ecosystems. These plants and microbes can break down pollutants, absorb excess nutrients, and rebuild the natural filtration systems of wetlands, allowing them to function as vital ecosystems once again.

Perhaps one of the most radical developments in restoration technology is the concept of de-extinction—the process of bringing back species that have gone extinct using synthetic biology. While still in its early stages, de-extinction efforts have focused on species like the woolly mammoth, with the goal of reintroducing these animals to ecosystems where they once played a key role. The idea is that by restoring these species, ecosystems that have been disrupted by their absence can be revitalized.

## The New Ecology: Human and Nature in Symbiosis

The advances in bioengineering and synthetic biology described above have ushered in what can be called the New Ecology—a vision of a world where humans and nature exist in symbiosis, rather than in conflict. In the New Ecology, technology is not used to exploit or dominate nature, but to restore, enhance, and coexist with it.

This new relationship with nature is guided by the principles of regeneration and sustainability. Instead of extracting resources from the Earth and depleting ecosystems, bioengineered solutions are used to regenerate what has been lost. Cities become green, living ecosystems that contribute to the health of the planet. Agriculture becomes regenerative, restoring soil health and biodiversity rather than depleting it. Ecosystems that have been damaged by human activities are healed using bioengineered organisms designed to work with nature, not against it.

The New Ecology is also characterized by a profound rethinking of humanity's place in the natural world. Rather than seeing humans as separate from or above nature, the New Ecology emphasizes interdependence. Humans are part of nature, and the technologies we create can be used to enhance this relationship, rather than disrupt it. In this vision, technology becomes a tool for ecological stewardship, helping to manage ecosystems in ways that promote biodiversity, resilience, and sustainability.

This shift in perspective is also reflected in the rise of biomimicry—the design of technologies and systems that mimic natural processes. Biomimicry is based on the idea that nature, through billions of years of evolution, has already solved many of the challenges we face today. By studying and imitating nature, humans can develop technologies that are more efficient, sustainable, and harmonious with the environment.

For example, self-healing materials inspired by biological systems are being developed for use in construction and manufacturing. These materials can repair themselves when damaged, reducing the need for maintenance and extending their lifespan. Bionic systems, which integrate biological and technological components, are being used in fields ranging from medicine to architecture, creating solutions that blur the line between the natural and the artificial.

In the New Ecology, humans are no longer conquerors of nature but collaborators with it. Bioengineering and synthetic biology offer the tools to repair the damage of the past and create a future where technology and nature work together in harmony.

## Techno-Moral Dilemmas: Ethical Challenges Arising from the Integration of AI and Biotech into Human Life

Introduction to Techno-Moral Dilemmas

As AI and biotechnology become increasingly integrated into human life, they bring with them a host of ethical challenges and techno-moral dilemmas. These dilemmas arise from the complex and often unpredictable consequences of using advanced technologies to modify life, enhance human capabilities, and shape societal systems. While these technologies offer enormous potential to solve global challenges—such as climate change, disease, and food security—they also raise fundamental questions about autonomy, justice, equity, and the nature of human existence.

The techno-moral dilemmas of the Silicocene are not just theoretical debates for philosophers and ethicists; they have real-world implications that affect individuals, communities, and the planet. As AI systems take on more decision-making roles, and bioengineering redefines what it means to be human, society must grapple with the ethical challenges posed by these transformative technologies. How do we ensure that these technologies are used for the common good, rather than for exploitation or control? How do we navigate the risks of unintended consequences, from genetic manipulation to autonomous AI systems? And perhaps most fundamentally, what kind of future do we want to create as we integrate AI and biotech into the fabric of life?

## Autonomy and Human Enhancement: Redefining the Human Experience

One of the most profound ethical challenges posed by biotechnology and AI is the question of autonomy—the right of individuals to make decisions about their own bodies, minds, and lives. As biotech advances enable humans to enhance their physical and cognitive abilities, society must confront difficult questions about the limits of these enhancements and the impact they will have on human identity.

### Human Enhancement Technologies

Technologies such as genetic modification, brain-computer interfaces (BCIs), and cybernetic implants offer the potential to enhance human abilities beyond natural limits. Genetic modification, for example, can be used to eliminate genetic diseases or enhance physical traits, such as strength or intelligence. BCIs allow humans to interface directly with machines, enhancing cognitive abilities or even enabling new forms of communication. Cybernetic implants can enhance sensory perception, restore mobility to the disabled, or improve physical performance.

While these technologies have the potential to greatly improve human life, they also raise ethical questions about what it means to be human. If we can genetically engineer our children to be smarter, stronger, or more attractive, do we risk creating a society of genetic elites who have unfair advantages over those who cannot afford or access these enhancements? Will human diversity and individuality be lost as people choose to enhance themselves in similar ways, leading to a kind of technological homogenization?

The concept of autonomy is also challenged by the integration of AI systems into human bodies and minds. BCIs, for example, offer the potential to merge human consciousness with machine intelligence, creating cyborg entities that blur the line between human and machine. While these technologies could greatly expand human capabilities, they also raise concerns about control and manipulation. If AI systems are capable of influencing human thoughts or decisions through BCIs, where does the boundary between human autonomy and machine influence lie?

Cognitive Liberty and the Right to Choose

As human enhancement technologies become more advanced, questions of cognitive liberty—the right to control one's own mental processes and identity—become increasingly important. Individuals should have the freedom to choose whether or not to enhance themselves, but societal pressures, economic incentives, and the competitive nature of hypercapitalism may push people toward enhancement even if they would otherwise prefer to remain unmodified.

For example, in a future where enhanced intelligence is common, those who choose not to undergo cognitive enhancement may be at a significant disadvantage in the job market, education, or social status. This could create a new form of coercion, where people feel compelled to modify themselves to keep up with societal expectations, even if they have ethical or personal reservations about doing so.

The ethical principle of informed consent is also critical in the context of human enhancement. Individuals must be fully informed about the risks, benefits, and long-term consequences of enhancement technologies before making decisions about their use. This becomes more complex when dealing with technologies that involve altering the brain or genetic code, as the full implications of these changes may not be understood for generations.

AI Governance and the Challenge of Alignment

Another major ethical challenge in the Silicocene is the governance of artificial intelligence systems. As AI becomes more autonomous and more deeply integrated into human decision-making, ensuring that AI systems align with human values and ethics becomes increasingly important. This challenge is often referred to as the AI alignment problem—the task of designing AI systems that act in ways that are consistent with human goals, values, and well-being.

Autonomous AI Systems and Ethical Decision-Making

One of the key concerns in AI ethics is the rise of autonomous AI systems that can make decisions without human oversight. These systems are increasingly used in areas such as healthcare, law enforcement, and finance, where they have the potential to improve efficiency and accuracy. However, autonomous AI systems also raise significant ethical risks, particularly when it comes to accountability and responsibility.

For example, in healthcare, AI systems are being used to assist doctors in diagnosing diseases and recommending treatments. While these systems can analyze vast amounts of data and identify patterns that humans might miss, they are not infallible. If an AI system makes an incorrect diagnosis that leads to harm, who is responsible? Is it the developer who created the AI, the healthcare provider who used it, or the AI system itself?

The challenge of ethical decision-making is even more acute in fields such as law enforcement and military applications, where AI systems are being used to make decisions about the use of force or surveillance. Autonomous drones, for example, are capable of identifying and engaging targets without direct human input. This raises serious ethical questions about the use of lethal force and the potential for unintended consequences.

To address these concerns, there is growing interest in developing ethical frameworks for AI governance. These frameworks seek to ensure that AI systems are designed and used in ways that respect human rights, promote fairness, and avoid harm. Key principles include transparency, accountability, and bias mitigation. AI developers are increasingly required to demonstrate how their systems make decisions, what data they are trained on, and how they mitigate potential biases.

However, the rapid pace of AI development often outstrips the ability of governments and institutions to regulate its use. International cooperation and AI governance mechanisms will be critical to ensuring that AI systems are aligned with global ethical standards and do not exacerbate existing inequalities or create new forms of harm.

Bias and Discrimination in AI Systems

One of the most well-known ethical concerns in AI development is the issue of bias. AI systems are trained on data, and if that data reflects existing societal biases—such as racial, gender, or socioeconomic disparities—then the AI system may perpetuate or even amplify those biases in its decision-making.

For example, AI algorithms used in hiring processes have been found to favor certain demographic groups over others, reinforcing patterns of discrimination in the workplace. Similarly, AI systems used in law enforcement may disproportionately target marginalized communities if they are trained on biased data from historical policing practices.

To address these issues, AI developers are increasingly focused on creating fair and transparent algorithms. This includes auditing AI systems for bias, ensuring that diverse data sets are used for training, and involving ethicists and social scientists in the development process. However, the challenge of bias in AI remains a significant ethical concern, particularly as AI systems are used in more critical and high-stakes decisions.

Bioethics and the Limits of Genetic Engineering

While AI raises questions about decision-making and governance, biotechnology, particularly in the field of genetic engineering, presents its own set of ethical challenges. The ability to modify the genetic code of organisms, including humans, opens up new possibilities for curing diseases, enhancing abilities, and even creating new forms of life. However, it also raises deep ethical questions about the limits of human intervention in nature and the potential consequences of genetic manipulation.

Germline Editing and Genetic Legacy

One of the most controversial areas of genetic engineering is germline editing—the process of making genetic modifications that are passed on to future generations. Germline editing has the potential to eliminate genetic diseases, such as cystic fibrosis or sickle cell anemia, from the human population. However, it also raises significant ethical concerns about genetic determinism and the potential for unintended consequences.

When genetic modifications are made to an individual's germline, those changes are inherited by their offspring and all future descendants. This means that decisions made by one generation could have far-reaching consequences for future generations, without their consent. There is also the risk of off-target effects, where genetic modifications intended to treat one condition could inadvertently cause other health problems.

The ethical principle of informed consent is particularly complex in the context of germline editing. Future generations cannot consent to the genetic modifications made by their ancestors, raising questions about the rights of individuals to control their own genetic inheritance. Additionally, the use of germline editing for non-therapeutic purposes—such as enhancing intelligence, physical appearance, or athletic ability—raises concerns about eugenics and the potential for genetic inequality.

Genetic Privacy and Ownership

Another ethical challenge in the field of genetic engineering is the issue of genetic privacy and ownership. As genetic sequencing becomes more widespread, individuals' genetic information is increasingly stored in databases used for research, healthcare, and even law enforcement. This raises concerns about data privacy and the potential misuse of genetic information.

For example, insurance companies could potentially use genetic information to deny coverage or charge higher premiums to individuals with certain genetic predispositions. Law enforcement agencies could use genetic databases to track individuals or solve crimes, raising concerns about genetic surveillance and privacy violations.

The question of genetic ownership is also ethically complex. If a person's genetic information is used in research that leads to the development of a new drug or treatment, does that person have the right to share in the profits? Similarly, if a company patents a genetic modification or a synthetic organism, does that give them control over the use of that genetic material?

The Challenge of Ecological Balance and Bioengineering

As bioengineering becomes more integrated into environmental restoration and management, new ethical dilemmas arise around the concept of ecological balance. While bioengineered organisms offer the potential to restore damaged ecosystems, they also raise concerns about unintended ecological consequences and the risk of biological contamination.

The Risk of Unintended Ecological Consequences

One of the major ethical concerns with the use of bioengineered organisms in environmental restoration is the risk of unintended consequences. Ecosystems are complex, interconnected systems, and introducing new organisms—whether bioengineered plants, microbes, or animals—can have unpredictable effects on biodiversity, food chains, and ecosystem stability.

For example, bioengineered plants designed to absorb more carbon dioxide may outcompete native species, leading to a loss of biodiversity. Similarly, genetically modified microbes used to break down pollutants could spread beyond the intended area and disrupt natural microbial communities. The release of bioengineered organisms into the wild also raises the risk of horizontal gene transfer, where genetic material from bioengineered organisms is transferred to wild species, potentially creating new hybrid organisms with unknown ecological impacts.

To mitigate these risks, bioengineers must carefully consider the long-term ecological impacts of their interventions. This includes conducting thorough risk assessments, monitoring bioengineered organisms in the environment, and developing containment strategies to prevent unintended spread. However, the complexity of ecosystems means that even the best-intentioned interventions carry some degree of uncertainty.

The Ethics of Ecological Manipulation

The ability to bioengineer organisms for environmental restoration also raises deeper ethical questions about the limits of human intervention in nature. Should humans have the right to manipulate ecosystems to suit their needs, even if the goal is to restore balance and repair damage caused by human activity? Or does this level of intervention risk further disrupting the delicate balance of nature?

Some environmental ethicists argue that the use of bioengineering for restoration is a form of technological hubris—the belief that humans can control and manage nature in ways that are ultimately unsustainable. They advocate for a more hands-off approach to environmental restoration, allowing ecosystems to recover on their own without human intervention.

Others, however, argue that bioengineering is a necessary tool for addressing the unprecedented environmental challenges of the Anthropocene, and that ethical oversight can ensure that these technologies are used responsibly.

## Conclusion: Navigating the Techno-Moral Landscape of the Silicocene

The integration of AI and biotechnology into human life has opened up new possibilities for solving global challenges, enhancing human capabilities, and restoring ecosystems. However, these technologies also bring with them complex techno-moral dilemmas that require careful ethical consideration. From the governance of autonomous AI systems to the ethics of genetic enhancement and ecological manipulation, society must navigate a rapidly changing technological landscape while ensuring that human rights, autonomy, and environmental sustainability are upheld.

In the Silicocene, the relationship between technology and nature is no longer one of domination or exploitation, but of co-evolution and symbiosis. As humans become more intertwined with machines and bioengineered organisms, the ethical frameworks that guide technological development must evolve to reflect the new realities of life in this era. Ensuring that these technologies are aligned with the values of equity, sustainability, and collective well-being will be critical to creating a future where technology and nature coexist in harmony.

## The Societal Transformation in the Silicocene

The transition into the Silicocene, a new era marked by profound technological advancements and a redefined relationship with nature, also brings about a monumental transformation in human society. Central to this change is the shift away from the capitalist structures that dominated the Anthropocene toward new economic, social, and political models that prioritize sustainability, equity, and collective well-being. This societal transformation represents a move beyond hypercapitalism, with its inherent focus on profit and competition, toward systems that decentralize power, foster collaboration, and empower communities. The Silicocene creates the technological and cultural conditions for these new models to flourish, offering humanity a chance to rebuild society based on more equitable, regenerative, and distributed principles.

## Post-Hypercapitalism: The Emergence of New Economic Models

As humanity transitions into the Silicocene, the limitations and destructive tendencies of hypercapitalism—characterized by unregulated markets, unending consumption, and resource extraction—become increasingly apparent. Hypercapitalism, which fueled growth at the expense of the environment and social equity, is seen as incompatible with the urgent need to address climate change, resource depletion, and systemic inequality. The post-hypercapitalist society that emerges in the Silicocene is driven by a reimagining of economic systems, where the focus shifts from perpetual growth and profit maximization to sustainable, equitable, and regenerative modes of exchange.

In this new societal paradigm, three key economic models begin to take hold: circular economies, gift economies, and digital commons. Each of these models is enabled by the technological innovations and societal shifts that define the Silicocene, offering pathways to more sustainable and equitable futures.

The Circular Economy: Regeneration and Sustainability at the Core

One of the most prominent economic models to emerge in the post-hypercapitalist world is the circular economy, which moves away from the linear "take-make-dispose" model of production that dominated the Anthropocene. In a circular economy, resources are continuously cycled through systems of reuse, repair, and recycling, minimizing waste and the need for virgin materials. This model reflects the natural cycles found in ecosystems, where nothing is wasted and everything is repurposed. The circular economy is designed to be regenerative by design, focusing on the restoration of natural systems and the reduction of environmental impact.

The Silicocene, with its advances in biotechnology, artificial intelligence (AI), and robotics, enables circular economies to function on a scale previously unimaginable. For example, AI-driven systems can optimize supply chains to ensure that products are designed for durability, modularity, and repairability. Machine learning algorithms can track material flows through the economy, predicting when products will reach the end of their life cycle and facilitating their disassembly and reuse. Biotechnology allows for the development of bio-based materials that are fully biodegradable, ensuring that any waste generated by industrial processes can be safely returned to the environment as nutrients.

In this post-hypercapitalist society, businesses and industries no longer operate on a model of planned obsolescence, where products are designed to fail after a certain period to drive consumerism. Instead, companies focus on creating long-lasting, modular products that can be easily repaired or upgraded. Consumers are no longer simply buyers but participants in a system of shared ownership, where goods are rented, leased, or shared rather than owned outright. This shift is facilitated by digital platforms that track the lifecycle of products and coordinate their redistribution or repurposing when no longer needed by their original users.

One key example of this in the Silicocene is the concept of urban mining, where cities become sources of valuable materials, as opposed to traditional extraction from natural ecosystems. AI and robotic technologies are used to identify, recover, and recycle metals, plastics, and other valuable materials from old buildings, infrastructure, and consumer goods. This not only reduces the demand for new raw materials but also reduces the environmental footprint of resource extraction, contributing to a more sustainable relationship between society and the planet.

Moreover, closed-loop supply chains become standard practice, where industries take responsibility for the entire life cycle of their products, from design and production to disposal and regeneration. This shift encourages companies to use renewable energy, biodegradable materials, and design principles that prioritize longevity and repairability. By reducing waste and ensuring that resources remain in circulation for as long as possible, the circular economy contributes to a more sustainable, resilient, and regenerative society.

## The Gift Economy: Building a Society Based on Generosity and Reciprocity

In addition to the rise of circular economies, the post-hypercapitalist world of the Silicocene sees the resurgence of gift economies—economic systems based on generosity, reciprocity, and communal exchange rather than monetary transactions. While gift economies have existed in various forms throughout human history, technological advances and societal shifts in the Silicocene enable these systems to thrive on a much larger scale.

In a gift economy, goods, services, and resources are shared freely within a community, without the expectation of direct compensation. Instead of transactions being mediated by money, exchanges are based on social bonds, trust, and mutual aid. This model fosters a sense of community solidarity and reduces dependence on hierarchical, profit-driven economic structures. People contribute to the well-being of others based on their abilities and resources, and in return, they receive what they need from the collective.

The digital platforms and blockchain technologies that characterize the Silicocene provide the infrastructure for large-scale gift economies to function efficiently. For example, decentralized networks facilitate peer-to-peer exchanges of goods and services, allowing people to share resources like housing, food, and tools with others in their community or even across global networks. Blockchain ensures transparency and trust in these transactions by creating verifiable records of contributions and exchanges, reducing the potential for exploitation or inequality.

Gift economies are particularly well-suited to addressing the challenges of scarcity in the post-hypercapitalist world, where access to essential resources like clean water, food, and energy may be limited in some regions. In these contexts, communities rely on gift-based systems of mutual aid to ensure that everyone's needs are met, without the need for centralized authorities or market-driven mechanisms. This fosters local resilience and ensures that communities can support themselves in times of crisis.

An example of the gift economy in action is the rise of community-based agriculture systems, where individuals contribute their labor, land, or knowledge to grow food for the entire community. These systems emphasize local food production, reducing reliance on industrial agriculture and long-distance supply chains. The surplus food is shared freely within the community, with no expectation of payment or compensation, reinforcing bonds of trust and cooperation.

The gift economy also plays a crucial role in the cultural transformation of the Silicocene. As society shifts away from consumerism and materialism, people place greater value on relationships, experiences, and communal well-being. Festivals, celebrations, and cultural exchanges become important ways for people to express generosity and strengthen social bonds. In these contexts, gifts are not just material goods but also acts of service, knowledge sharing, and creative expression, contributing to a richer, more connected society.

The Digital Commons: A Shared Knowledge Economy

Another key feature of the post-hypercapitalist society in the Silicocene is the rise of the digital commons—shared digital resources, knowledge, and infrastructure that are collectively owned and managed by communities rather than controlled by private corporations or governments. The digital commons represent a fundamental shift away from the privatization and commodification of knowledge that characterized the hypercapitalist era. Instead, information, software, and other digital resources are treated as public goods, accessible to all and governed by principles of openness, collaboration, and transparency.

The open-source movement, which began in the late 20th century, laid the groundwork for the digital commons, demonstrating that software and knowledge could be developed collaboratively and shared freely. In the Silicocene, this ethos extends far beyond software, encompassing a wide range of digital resources, from AI models to scientific research, educational materials, and even the genetic codes of bioengineered organisms.

Blockchain technology plays a central role in the governance and management of the digital commons. By enabling decentralized and transparent systems of record-keeping, blockchain allows communities to collectively manage digital resources without the need for centralized authorities or intermediaries. This ensures that the digital commons remain open, accessible, and accountable to the communities that rely on them.

One of the most significant aspects of the digital commons is the open access to knowledge and innovation. In contrast to the proprietary, patent-driven systems of the hypercapitalist era, where innovation was controlled by a few powerful corporations, the digital commons allow anyone with access to the internet to contribute to and benefit from collective knowledge. Open-source AI models, for example, can be used and modified by researchers, developers, and communities around the world, accelerating innovation and ensuring that the benefits of AI are widely distributed.

The digital commons also play a crucial role in promoting social equity and inclusion. By providing free and open access to educational materials, digital tools, and technological infrastructure, the digital commons help bridge the digital divide and empower marginalized communities. In the post-hypercapitalist world, access to the digital commons is seen as a fundamental human right, ensuring that everyone has the opportunity to participate in the knowledge economy and contribute to the collective well-being of society.

Commons-based peer production is another key aspect of the digital commons. This refers to the collaborative production of goods and services by self-organizing communities, often without the need for financial compensation. The Wikipedia model, where thousands of volunteers contribute to the creation and maintenance of a free and open encyclopedia, is a prime example of this form of production. In the Silicocene, commons-based peer production extends to a wide range of sectors, from software development to renewable energy systems, healthcare solutions, and scientific research.

In this new economic paradigm, value is not measured solely in terms of monetary profit but in terms of the social and ecological benefits that are generated by collective efforts. The digital commons enable communities to pool their knowledge, skills, and resources to solve complex challenges, from climate change to public health, without the constraints of profit-driven market forces.

---

## Decentralization and Empowerment: Reshaping Power Structures in the Silicocene

In the post-hypercapitalist society of the Silicocene, the decentralization of power becomes a central theme in both economic and political life. The hypercentralized institutions of the Anthropocene—multinational corporations, nation-states, and financial markets—are gradually replaced by decentralized networks and systems that distribute power more equitably across society. This decentralization is driven by technological innovations such as blockchain, decentralized AI, and localism, which enable communities to reclaim agency and control over their economic, political, and social lives.

Blockchain: A Framework for Decentralized Governance and Trust

One of the most transformative technologies driving decentralization in the Silicocene is blockchain. Initially developed as the underlying technology for cryptocurrencies like Bitcoin, blockchain has evolved into a powerful tool for creating trustless, decentralized networks that enable transparent and accountable governance. Blockchain's decentralized nature eliminates the need for intermediaries—such as banks, governments, or corporations—by providing a secure, distributed ledger that records transactions and agreements in a verifiable and immutable way.

In the Silicocene, blockchain technology is applied to a wide range of sectors, from finance and supply chains to healthcare and governance. It allows communities to create decentralized autonomous organizations (DAOs)—entities governed by smart contracts that are executed automatically based on pre-defined rules encoded into the blockchain. These DAOs are often used to manage collective resources, such as community energy grids, shared land, or digital commons, without the need for hierarchical leadership structures.

Blockchain's ability to create trust in decentralized systems is particularly important in the post-hypercapitalist world, where traditional institutions are no longer seen as reliable arbiters of power. In the Anthropocene, centralized institutions often acted in their own self-interest, contributing to corruption, inequality, and environmental degradation. Blockchain offers a way to rebuild trust through transparency and distributed accountability, ensuring that decision-making processes are open to scrutiny and cannot be manipulated by powerful elites.

One key example of blockchain's potential for decentralization is in the energy sector. In the Silicocene, decentralized energy grids are powered by renewable sources like solar and wind, with each household, business, or community able to generate and store its own energy. Blockchain-based systems allow these energy producers to trade electricity directly with one another, creating peer-to-peer energy markets without the need for utility companies or centralized power plants. This not only reduces reliance on fossil fuels but also empowers communities to take control of their energy systems.

Blockchain also plays a crucial role in democratic governance, enabling new forms of digital democracy where citizens can participate directly in decision-making processes. In these systems, blockchain ensures that votes are transparent, verifiable, and secure, reducing the risk of electoral fraud or manipulation. Smart contracts can be used to execute policies automatically once certain conditions are met, making governance more efficient and responsive to the needs of the community.

In the post-hypercapitalist world, blockchain becomes a tool for redistributing power and rebuilding trust in social systems, ensuring that resources, decision-making, and opportunities are shared more equitably across society.

Decentralized AI: Democratizing Intelligence and Decision-Making

While blockchain provides the infrastructure for decentralized governance, decentralized AI enables the democratization of intelligence and decision-making. In the hypercapitalist era, AI was largely controlled by a few powerful corporations that had access to the vast amounts of data needed to train advanced machine learning models. This concentration of AI power led to concerns about surveillance, privacy, and the monopolization of innovation.

In the Silicocene, the development of decentralized AI networks breaks this concentration of power by allowing individuals, communities, and organizations to collaboratively train and deploy AI models. Instead of relying on centralized data silos owned by corporations, decentralized AI networks are powered by distributed computing and federated learning. This approach allows AI models to be trained on data that is kept locally, ensuring that sensitive information never leaves the control of the individuals or organizations that own it. The result is a more privacy-preserving, transparent, and democratic AI ecosystem.

Decentralized AI has wide-ranging implications for society. In healthcare, for example, decentralized AI systems enable individuals to contribute their medical data to the training of AI models without having to share it with centralized institutions. This allows for the development of more accurate and personalized healthcare solutions while protecting patient privacy. Similarly, in agriculture, decentralized AI systems help farmers optimize crop yields and manage resources by aggregating data from local environments, without requiring them to give up control of their data to agribusinesses.

Moreover, decentralized AI systems can be used to automate decision-making in local governance, empowering communities to collectively manage their resources. For example, in urban planning, decentralized AI systems analyze data from sensors placed throughout a city to optimize traffic flows, reduce energy consumption, and improve public services. Because these AI systems are governed by the community, citizens have greater control over how the data is used and how decisions are made, leading to more inclusive and responsive urban management.

Decentralized AI also plays a key role in addressing inequality by providing access to advanced tools and technologies that were previously only available to large corporations or governments. In the post-hypercapitalist world, open-source AI models are freely available to individuals and small organizations, allowing them to innovate, solve problems, and create value without the need for large-scale capital investment.

## Localism: Empowering Communities and Building Resilience

At the heart of the societal transformation in the Silicocene is the rise of localism—the idea that power, resources, and decision-making should be returned to local communities rather than centralized in distant institutions. Localism is a response to the failures of hypercapitalism, where globalization and the concentration of wealth and power in urban centers often left rural areas and smaller communities marginalized and impoverished.

In the Silicocene, localism is enabled by technological innovations that allow communities to become more self-sufficient and resilient. Advances in 3D printing, renewable energy, urban agriculture, and decentralized networks mean that communities can produce much of what they need locally, reducing their reliance on global supply chains and multinational corporations. This shift toward local production and consumption fosters greater resilience in the face of global crises, such as pandemics, climate change, and economic shocks.

Community-based economies become the foundation of the post-hypercapitalist world. Local markets, cooperatives, and shared ownership models replace the extractive economies of the Anthropocene, where wealth was funneled away from local communities and into the hands of distant corporations. In this new model, wealth is generated and retained within the community, creating more equitable and sustainable economies.

Localism also emphasizes the importance of cultural and ecological diversity. Communities are encouraged to develop economic systems that reflect their unique ecological and cultural contexts, rather than conforming to the standardized, one-size-fits-all models of global capitalism. This leads to the resurgence of indigenous knowledge systems, traditional agricultural practices, and local governance structures that are better suited to the needs and values of each community.

Digital technologies play a crucial role in supporting localism by connecting local communities to global networks of knowledge, resources, and solidarity. While production and decision-making are localized, communities remain connected to the wider world through decentralized digital platforms that facilitate knowledge exchange, mutual aid, and collaboration. These platforms enable communities to share best practices, access open-source technologies, and build alliances with other like-minded groups.

The rise of localism also transforms political power structures. In the Silicocene, the nation-state loses much of its centralized authority, as decision-making is devolved to local councils, municipalities, and regional coalitions. These smaller governance units are better able to respond to the specific needs of their populations and ecosystems, fostering more participatory democracy and responsive governance. At the same time, local communities collaborate through global networks to address larger-scale challenges, such as climate change, ensuring that local solutions are informed by global knowledge and solidarity.

## Conclusion: The Societal Transformation of the Silicocene

The transition to the Silicocene represents a profound societal transformation, driven by the collapse of hypercapitalism and the rise of new economic models that prioritize sustainability, equity, and community well-being. In this post-hypercapitalist world, circular economies, gift economies, and digital commons replace the extractive and profit-driven systems of the past, creating a more regenerative and inclusive economy.

At the same time, the decentralization of power—enabled by technologies like blockchain, decentralized AI, and localism—reshapes political and economic structures, empowering communities to take control of their own resources and decision-making processes. This shift away from centralized authority and toward distributed, community-based systems fosters resilience, diversity, and cooperation in the face of global challenges.

In the Silicocene, society is no longer driven by the pursuit of endless growth and consumption. Instead, it is built on principles of sustainability, collaboration, and collective empowerment, offering humanity a chance to create a more just, resilient, and harmonious future. This societal transformation is not only a response to the failures of the Anthropocene but also a proactive reimagining of what is possible when technology and nature work in concert to support the well-being of all life on Earth.

## The Future of Work: How Automation and AI May Lead to Universal Basic Income (UBI), Shorter Work Weeks, and Creativity-Focused Economies

Introduction to the Future of Work in the Silicocene

As we enter the Silicocene era, a period characterized by the convergence of advanced technologies, automation, and artificial intelligence (AI), we are witnessing fundamental changes in the nature of work. In the Anthropocene, human labor was central to economic productivity, with the majority of people participating in labor-intensive industries such as agriculture, manufacturing, and services. However, the rapid advancement of AI and robotics is gradually transforming the workforce, with machines taking over tasks that were once performed by humans. This shift toward automation raises profound questions about the future of work, economic structures, and the well-being of workers.

Automation has the potential to significantly increase productivity and efficiency, but it also raises concerns about mass unemployment, income inequality, and social displacement. As jobs are increasingly automated, new economic models, such as universal basic income (UBI), shorter work weeks, and creativity-focused economies, are emerging as potential solutions to these challenges. These models represent a reimagining of labor, where the value of human work is not solely measured by its economic output, but also by its contribution to creativity, innovation, and personal fulfillment.

Automation and Job Displacement: The Challenges of the AI Revolution

The rise of automation and AI technologies is reshaping the global workforce in profound ways. Machines and AI systems are increasingly capable of performing tasks that require human intelligence, such as data analysis, pattern recognition, problem-solving, and even creative work. Industries such as manufacturing, logistics, healthcare, and retail are already seeing significant disruptions as robots and AI systems take over roles that were traditionally held by human workers.

In particular, routine and repetitive tasks are highly susceptible to automation. Jobs that involve physical labor, data entry, and basic decision-making are being replaced by robots and AI algorithms. For example, autonomous robots are now capable of assembling products on factory floors, AI-powered chatbots are handling customer service inquiries, and self-driving vehicles are revolutionizing the transportation industry.

However, the displacement of human workers by automation poses significant social and economic challenges. As machines take over more jobs, millions of workers may find themselves unemployed or underemployed, particularly those in low-skilled or middle-skilled roles. This has the potential to exacerbate existing inequalities, as marginalized communities and those with fewer educational opportunities are likely to be disproportionately affected.

To mitigate the negative effects of automation, societies must explore new economic models and social safety nets that ensure economic security and well-being for all individuals, regardless of their employment status. One of the most prominent solutions being discussed is the implementation of universal basic income (UBI), a policy that provides individuals with a guaranteed, unconditional income regardless of their work status.

Universal Basic Income (UBI): A Safety Net for the Age of Automation

Universal basic income (UBI) is a revolutionary concept that has gained significant attention in the context of automation and AI-driven job displacement. The idea behind UBI is simple: every individual, regardless of employment status, receives a regular, unconditional cash payment from the government. This payment is designed to provide a basic level of economic security, ensuring that individuals can meet their basic needs even if they are unable to find traditional employment.

The potential benefits of UBI in a world dominated by automation are numerous. First and foremost, UBI serves as a safety net for workers who lose their jobs due to automation. By providing individuals with a stable source of income, UBI can help alleviate poverty, reduce inequality, and prevent the social unrest that may arise from mass unemployment. Moreover, UBI has the potential to reduce stress and improve mental health, as individuals are no longer constantly worried about job security and financial survival.

However, UBI is not without its critics. Some argue that providing a guaranteed income could disincentivize work, leading to reduced productivity and economic stagnation. Others raise concerns about the fiscal sustainability of UBI, questioning how governments would fund such a program, particularly in countries with large populations. Despite these concerns, several pilot programs and experiments have shown promising results, with UBI recipients reporting higher levels of happiness, creativity, and entrepreneurial activity.

In the context of the Silicocene, where automation is expected to replace a significant portion of the workforce, UBI could become a central pillar of a new economic model. By decoupling income from traditional employment, UBI allows individuals to pursue activities that may not have been financially viable in the past, such as creative endeavors, community-building, and lifelong learning. This shift toward a post-work society could foster a more innovative, equitable, and inclusive economy.

## Shorter Work Weeks: Rethinking Productivity and Well-Being

Another potential outcome of the automation revolution is the adoption of shorter work weeks. As AI and automation increase productivity, fewer human workers are needed to produce the same amount of goods and services. This opens the door to reducing the number of hours individuals spend working, without sacrificing economic output. In the Silicocene, a four-day work week or even a three-day work week could become the norm, allowing individuals to spend more time on activities that enhance their quality of life.

The idea of shorter work weeks is not new. In fact, many labor movements throughout history have fought for reduced working hours, with the goal of improving workers' well-being and promoting work-life balance. In the 20th century, the transition from six-day work weeks to five-day work weeks was a major victory for labor rights. Today, the conversation around shorter work weeks is gaining renewed attention, particularly in the context of burnout, mental health, and the future of work.

Research has shown that long working hours are associated with higher levels of stress, anxiety, and depression, while shorter work weeks have been linked to improved productivity, job satisfaction, and work-life balance. By reducing the number of hours people spend working, societies can create more opportunities for individuals to engage in leisure activities, creativity, and community involvement.

In the Silicocene, where automation takes over many of the tasks that were once performed by human workers, the need for long work weeks diminishes. AI systems and robots can operate 24/7, ensuring that productivity remains high even as human workers spend less time on the job. This shift opens the door to a new way of thinking about work—one that prioritizes well-being, happiness, and creativity over economic output.

Governments and companies in the Silicocene may implement shorter work weeks as a way to promote social well-being and address the challenges of automation-induced unemployment. By reducing the number of hours individuals are expected to work, societies can redistribute labor more equitably, ensuring that everyone has the opportunity to contribute meaningfully to the economy while also enjoying more free time.

Creativity-Focused Economies: Valuing Human Innovation and Expression

One of the most exciting possibilities in the Silicocene is the emergence of creativity-focused economies, where human work is no longer centered on repetitive tasks or economic productivity, but rather on innovation, creativity, and personal expression. As automation takes over routine and labor-intensive jobs, humans are freed to pursue activities that require emotional intelligence, artistic expression, and creative problem-solving—areas where AI and robots are less effective.

In a creativity-focused economy, individuals are encouraged to explore their passions and talents in fields such as art, music, literature, design, and social entrepreneurship. AI systems can serve as collaborators, providing tools and insights that enhance human creativity, rather than replacing it. For example, AI algorithms can generate new musical compositions, suggest design elements for architectural projects, or assist writers in brainstorming ideas for novels.

The shift toward a creativity-focused economy also has profound implications for education and skills development. In the Silicocene, education systems may prioritize creative thinking, emotional intelligence, and interdisciplinary learning over traditional rote memorization and standardized testing. Schools and universities would focus on fostering innovation, collaboration, and problem-solving skills, preparing individuals for a future where creativity is the primary driver of economic and social value.

Moreover, the creativity-focused economy is not limited to traditional artistic fields. In sectors such as healthcare, urban planning, and environmental conservation, creative solutions are needed to address complex challenges. AI and automation can take over routine tasks in these fields, allowing human workers to focus on strategic decision-making, empathetic care, and innovative problem-solving.

In this new economic paradigm, value creation is no longer measured solely by economic output or financial profit. Instead, value is generated through social impact, cultural enrichment, and personal fulfillment. Governments and companies may invest in public programs and initiatives that support creative industries, social enterprises, and community projects, recognizing that these activities contribute to a more vibrant, inclusive, and resilient society.

Conclusion: The Future of Work in the Silicocene

The future of work in the Silicocene is shaped by the transformative power of AI and automation. As machines take over routine and repetitive tasks, human workers are freed to explore new forms of work that prioritize creativity, well-being, and social impact. Universal basic income (UBI) provides economic security in an era of job displacement, while shorter work weeks allow individuals to enjoy a better balance between work and leisure. At the same time, creativity-focused economies emerge as the driving force of the post-automation world, where human innovation and expression are valued above economic productivity.

In this new paradigm, work is no longer a means of survival but a path to personal fulfillment and collective flourishing. The future of work in the Silicocene offers a vision of a society where technology and humanity coexist harmoniously, creating opportunities for individuals to contribute meaningfully to the world while enjoying the fruits of a more equitable, inclusive, and sustainable economy.

## Equity and Justice in the Silicocene: Ensuring Marginalized Communities Benefit from Technological Shifts

Introduction: Equity and Justice in a Technologically Transformed World

The rise of advanced technologies such as AI, automation, and biotechnology has the potential to create tremendous benefits for society, from increased productivity to breakthroughs in healthcare and environmental conservation. However, these technologies also have the potential to exacerbate existing inequalities and further marginalize vulnerable communities. In the Silicocene, a key challenge is ensuring that the benefits of technological advancements are distributed equitably and that marginalized groups—such as people of color, low-income communities, Indigenous peoples, and women—are not left behind in the rapidly evolving technological landscape.

Equity and justice in the Silicocene require more than just access to technology. They demand systemic changes that address the root causes of inequality, including structural racism, gender discrimination, and economic disparities. Technological progress must be accompanied by policies, governance systems, and ethical frameworks that prioritize inclusion, social justice, and human rights.

This section explores the challenges and solutions related to ensuring that marginalized communities benefit from technological shifts in the Silicocene. It examines issues such as the digital divide, algorithmic bias, access to education and healthcare, and the role of community empowerment in promoting equity and justice.

The Digital Divide: Ensuring Equal Access to Technology

One of the most pressing challenges in achieving equity in the Silicocene is addressing the digital divide—the gap between those who have access to digital technologies and those who do not. As AI, automation, and digital platforms become increasingly central to economic and social life, individuals and communities without access to these technologies are at risk of being further marginalized.

The digital divide is particularly pronounced along lines of race, income, and geography. In both developed and developing countries, low-income communities, rural areas, and communities of color often have less access to high-speed internet, digital devices, and the skills needed to participate in the digital economy. This lack of access limits their ability to benefit from advancements in education, healthcare, employment, and social services.

To ensure equity in the Silicocene, governments and organizations must prioritize efforts to close the digital divide. This can be achieved through a combination of infrastructure investments, digital literacy programs, and policies that promote affordable access to technology. For example, governments can invest in broadband infrastructure in underserved rural areas, ensuring that all communities have access to high-speed internet. Public-private partnerships can also play a role in providing affordable digital devices to low-income families.

In addition to providing access to technology, digital literacy is essential for ensuring that marginalized communities can fully participate in the digital economy. Digital literacy programs should be designed to teach individuals not only how to use technology but also how to critically engage with digital platforms, protect their privacy, and navigate the risks of online spaces. These programs should be accessible to people of all ages and backgrounds, with a particular focus on empowering women, youth, and communities of color.

Algorithmic Bias: Addressing Discrimination in AI Systems

As AI systems become more integrated into decision-making processes in areas such as healthcare, criminal justice, hiring, and finance, concerns about algorithmic bias and discrimination have come to the forefront. AI systems are trained on large datasets, and if these datasets reflect historical biases—such as racial or gender discrimination—the AI systems may perpetuate or even amplify these biases in their decision-making.

For example, studies have shown that facial recognition systems are less accurate in identifying people of color, leading to higher rates of false positives and false negatives for marginalized groups. Similarly, AI algorithms used in hiring processes may favor certain demographic groups over others, reinforcing existing patterns of discrimination in the workforce. In the criminal justice system, AI-driven predictive policing algorithms have been found to disproportionately target Black and brown communities, leading to over-policing and mass incarceration.

To address these challenges, developers of AI systems must prioritize fairness, transparency, and accountability in the design and deployment of their technologies. This includes conducting bias audits to identify and mitigate potential sources of discrimination in AI algorithms. It also requires the use of diverse and representative datasets in training AI models, ensuring that the systems do not reinforce existing inequalities.

In addition to technical solutions, regulatory frameworks are needed to ensure that AI systems are held to high ethical standards. Governments should implement policies that require companies and organizations to be transparent about how their AI systems make decisions and to provide mechanisms for individuals to challenge decisions made by AI. These frameworks should also include anti-discrimination laws that protect individuals from biased AI systems, similar to existing laws that prohibit discrimination in hiring, housing, and public services.

Achieving equity in the age of AI requires a commitment to ethical AI development and social justice. By addressing algorithmic bias and ensuring that AI systems are fair and inclusive, society can create a future where technology serves the common good and uplifts marginalized communities.

Access to Education and Healthcare: Bridging Gaps in Essential Services

In the Silicocene, access to education and healthcare is increasingly mediated by digital technologies and AI-driven systems. While these technologies have the potential to improve access to high-quality education and healthcare for all individuals, they also risk deepening existing inequalities if marginalized communities are excluded from these services.

Education in the Silicocene is undergoing a transformation, with the rise of online learning platforms, AI-driven personalized learning, and digital classrooms. These technologies can provide students with access to a wealth of knowledge, tailored learning experiences, and opportunities for collaboration across geographic boundaries. However, without efforts to ensure universal access to these technologies, students from low-income communities, rural areas, and marginalized groups may be left behind.

To promote equity in education, governments and organizations must invest in ensuring that all students have access to digital devices, internet connectivity, and the skills needed to succeed in a digital learning environment. This includes providing subsidies or free access to digital devices for low-income families, expanding broadband infrastructure in underserved areas, and offering digital literacy training for students and educators.

Healthcare is another critical area where technological advancements have the potential to improve equity. AI-driven systems can analyze medical data to provide personalized treatments, predict health outcomes, and improve diagnostic accuracy. Telemedicine platforms can connect patients in remote areas with healthcare providers, overcoming geographic barriers to care. However, the benefits of AI-driven healthcare are not evenly distributed, with marginalized communities often facing barriers to accessing these services.

To address these challenges, healthcare systems must be designed with equity in mind. This includes ensuring that AI systems used in healthcare are trained on diverse datasets that reflect the needs and experiences of different populations. Healthcare providers must also prioritize cultural competence and language accessibility in the design of digital health platforms, ensuring that patients from diverse backgrounds can fully engage with their healthcare providers.

Furthermore, policies that promote universal healthcare access are essential to ensuring that marginalized communities benefit from technological advancements in healthcare. This may include expanding public healthcare programs, providing subsidies for telemedicine services, and ensuring that healthcare providers in underserved areas have access to the latest AI-driven diagnostic tools.

Community Empowerment: Building Inclusive and Participatory Systems

One of the most important aspects of achieving equity and justice in the Silicocene is the empowerment of marginalized communities to actively participate in decision-making processes related to technology development and deployment. Too often, decisions about the use of advanced technologies are made by governments, corporations, and technologists without meaningful input from the communities that will be most affected by these technologies.

To address this power imbalance, new models of participatory governance and community-driven innovation must be developed. This includes creating spaces where marginalized communities can co-design and co-govern technologies that impact their lives. For example, communities should be involved in the development of smart city technologies, ensuring that the deployment of AI and digital infrastructure aligns with their needs and values. Similarly, Indigenous communities should have a say in the use of biotechnology and AI systems in environmental conservation efforts, recognizing their traditional knowledge and expertise in land stewardship.

Citizen assemblies, community boards, and participatory budgeting processes can provide platforms for marginalized communities to have a voice in technological governance. These models promote inclusive decision-making and ensure that the benefits of technological advancements are shared equitably.

In addition to participatory governance, education and capacity-building programs are essential for empowering marginalized communities to engage with technology. This includes providing training in digital skills, data literacy, and AI ethics, as well as supporting the development of community-based technology projects. By building the capacity of marginalized communities to understand and shape the technologies that impact their lives, society can create a more just and inclusive technological landscape.

Conclusion: Equity and Justice in the Silicocene

Achieving equity and justice in the Silicocene requires a multi-faceted approach that addresses the digital divide, algorithmic bias, and access to essential services such as education and healthcare. It also requires the empowerment of marginalized communities to participate in decision-making processes related to technology development and deployment. By prioritizing inclusion, social justice, and human rights, society can ensure that the benefits of technological advancements are shared equitably and that marginalized groups are not left behind in the rapidly evolving technological landscape.

## Political Structures in the Silicocene: Governance, Democracy, and Global Cooperation

Introduction: The Transformation of Governance in the Silicocene

The rise of advanced technologies such as AI, automation, and blockchain is not only transforming economic systems and the nature of work but also reshaping political structures and governance models in the Silicocene. As societies become more interconnected and reliant on digital technologies, traditional forms of governance—characterized by centralized authority and bureaucratic institutions—are increasingly seen as inadequate for addressing the complex challenges of the 21st century, such as climate change, inequality, and global health crises.

In response, new governance systems are emerging that prioritize decentralization, participatory democracy, and global cooperation. These systems leverage the power of digital platforms, AI, and blockchain to create more transparent, responsive, and inclusive political structures. At the same time, the rise of global challenges that transcend national borders is driving the need for new forms of international cooperation and global governance that can effectively address issues such as climate change, pandemics, and cybersecurity.

This section explores the political structures that may emerge in the Silicocene, focusing on the role of technology in shaping democracy, participation, and global cooperation. It examines how blockchain and decentralized governance models can empower citizens, how AI can be used to improve decision-making, and how international organizations can promote peace, sustainability, and human rights in an increasingly interconnected world.

Decentralized Governance: Empowering Communities through Blockchain and DAOs

One of the most significant trends in political structures in the Silicocene is the rise of decentralized governance models that redistribute power from centralized authorities to local communities and individuals. Blockchain technology plays a central role in this transformation, providing the infrastructure for decentralized autonomous organizations (DAOs) and other forms of distributed governance.

DAOs are blockchain-based entities that operate according to predefined rules encoded in smart contracts. These smart contracts automatically execute decisions based on the collective will of the members of the DAO, without the need for hierarchical leadership structures. This decentralized model of governance allows for more transparent, efficient, and accountable decision-making, as all actions and transactions are recorded on the blockchain and can be audited by anyone.

In the Silicocene, DAOs are used to govern a wide range of entities, from local communities and cooperatives to global organizations and public institutions. For example, a city may use a DAO to manage its public infrastructure, with citizens voting on how to allocate resources for public transportation, green spaces, and renewable energy projects. Similarly, global environmental organizations may use DAOs to coordinate climate action, with stakeholders from around the world participating in decision-making processes.

The transparency and accountability provided by blockchain technology help rebuild trust in political institutions, which have often been seen as corrupt or ineffective in the hypercapitalist era. By decentralizing governance and giving individuals a direct say in decision-making, DAOs empower citizens to take control of their communities and create more responsive and inclusive governance structures.

However, the rise of decentralized governance also raises important questions about representation, equity, and power dynamics. While blockchain technology can enhance transparency, it is not immune to the influence of powerful stakeholders who may seek to dominate decision-making processes. Ensuring that DAOs and other decentralized governance models are designed to be inclusive and representative of all members of society is essential for promoting equity and justice in the Silicocene.

Digital Democracy: Technology-Enhanced Participation and Decision-Making

The integration of digital technologies into governance systems is also transforming democracy and political participation. In the Silicocene, traditional forms of representative democracy—where citizens elect officials to make decisions on their behalf—are increasingly complemented by digital democracy, where citizens participate directly in decision-making through online platforms and digital tools.

Digital democracy leverages technologies such as AI, blockchain, and social media to create more transparent, inclusive, and participatory political systems. For example, AI-driven platforms can analyze public opinion and facilitate deliberative processes where citizens engage in discussions, debates, and voting on policy issues. Blockchain ensures that votes are secure, transparent, and verifiable, reducing the risk of electoral fraud and manipulation.

One of the key benefits of digital democracy is that it allows for real-time participation in governance, enabling citizens to have a direct say in the decisions that affect their lives. Instead of waiting for periodic elections, citizens can participate in continuous decision-making on a wide range of issues, from local infrastructure projects to national policies on healthcare and education. This creates a more dynamic and responsive form of democracy that is better suited to the fast-paced, interconnected world of the Silicocene.

Digital democracy also has the potential to empower marginalized groups that have historically been excluded from traditional political processes. By providing online platforms for political participation, digital democracy can reduce barriers to entry for individuals who may be unable to attend in-person meetings or who face discrimination in traditional political institutions. These platforms can also facilitate the formation of grassroots movements and social justice campaigns, giving marginalized communities a voice in shaping policies that affect their lives.

However, digital democracy also raises challenges related to privacy, surveillance, and digital literacy. As more political processes move online, there is a risk that citizens' data may be exploited by governments or corporations for purposes of surveillance or manipulation. Ensuring that digital democracy platforms are designed with privacy protections and data sovereignty in mind is essential for building trust and ensuring that citizens can participate freely and safely in the political process.

AI-Driven Governance: Improving Decision-Making and Public Services

In addition to blockchain and digital democracy, AI-driven governance is emerging as a powerful tool for improving decision-making and public services in the Silicocene. AI systems are increasingly used to analyze large datasets, identify patterns, and make predictions that can inform policy decisions and optimize the delivery of public services.

For example, AI systems can analyze data on transportation networks, energy consumption, and public health to help governments allocate resources more efficiently and reduce waste. In the context of climate change, AI-driven governance can be used to model the impact of different environmental policies, allowing governments to make more informed decisions about how to reduce carbon emissions and promote sustainability.

AI systems can also be used to improve the delivery of public services by automating routine tasks and reducing administrative burdens. For example, AI chatbots can provide citizens with information about government programs, process applications for social services, and handle inquiries from the public. This frees up human workers to focus on more complex tasks and provides citizens with faster and more efficient services.

However, the use of AI in governance also raises important ethical questions about accountability and transparency. As AI systems take on more decision-making roles, there is a risk that human oversight may be reduced, leading to decisions that are opaque or difficult to challenge. Ensuring that AI systems are transparent, auditable, and subject to human oversight is essential for building trust in AI-driven governance.

Moreover, the use of AI in governance must be guided by principles of fairness and equity. AI systems are only as good as the data they are trained on, and if that data reflects historical biases, the AI systems may perpetuate those biases in their decision-making. To address this challenge, governments must prioritize bias mitigation and inclusive data collection in the development of AI-driven governance systems.

Global Cooperation: Addressing Transnational Challenges in the Silicocene

The challenges of the 21st century—such as climate change, pandemics, cybersecurity, and migration—are transnational in nature, requiring global cooperation and international governance to address. In the Silicocene, the rise of advanced technologies and interconnected systems makes global cooperation more critical than ever, as issues that affect one part of the world can quickly ripple across borders.

One of the key innovations in global governance in the Silicocene is the use of digital platforms and AI-driven systems to facilitate international cooperation. For example, blockchain-based platforms can be used to create transparent and accountable systems for tracking carbon emissions, ensuring that countries meet their climate targets. AI systems can model the impact of different climate policies and recommend strategies for reducing emissions at a global scale.

In the context of global health, digital platforms and AI systems can be used to track the spread of diseases, predict outbreaks, and coordinate international responses. For example, during the COVID-19 pandemic, AI systems were used to analyze data on infection rates, hospital capacity, and vaccine distribution, helping governments make more informed decisions about how to respond to the crisis. In the Silicocene, these systems will become even more sophisticated, allowing for real-time monitoring and response to global health challenges.

International organizations such as the United Nations and the World Health Organization will play a critical role in facilitating global cooperation in the Silicocene. However, these organizations must evolve to keep pace with the rapidly changing technological landscape. This may include adopting digital governance models that allow for more inclusive and participatory decision-making, as well as leveraging AI and blockchain to improve transparency and accountability.

At the same time, the rise of decentralized governance models and global digital platforms raises questions about the role of nation-states in the Silicocene. As power becomes more distributed and global challenges require transnational solutions, the traditional model of sovereign nation-states may need to be reimagined. In the Silicocene, new forms of regional governance and global networks may emerge that allow for more flexible, responsive, and collaborative governance structures.

Conclusion: Political Structures in the Silicocene

The political structures of the Silicocene are shaped by the transformative power of digital technologies, AI, and blockchain. As societies become more interconnected and reliant on these technologies, traditional forms of governance are evolving into more decentralized, transparent, and participatory systems. Blockchain-based DAOs empower communities to take control of their own governance, while digital democracy platforms enhance political participation and make decision-making more responsive to the needs of citizens.

At the same time, AI-driven governance improves the efficiency and effectiveness of public services, while raising important ethical questions about accountability, transparency, and fairness. Global cooperation is essential for addressing transnational challenges, and digital platforms and AI systems provide new tools for facilitating international collaboration and ensuring that global governance is more inclusive and equitable.

In the Silicocene, political structures are no longer confined to the rigid hierarchies of the past. Instead, they are fluid, dynamic, and distributed, reflecting the complex and interconnected world in which we live. By embracing these new governance models, society can build a more just, inclusive, and resilient future, where technology serves the common good and empowers individuals and communities to shape their own destinies.

# Chapter 5: Harmonizing with Nature - The Age of Symbiosis

As we transition into the Silicocene—the age where humanity, artificial intelligence, and technology reach a new equilibrium—the possibility of a harmonious coexistence with nature becomes more than just a vision. It becomes a reality. This age, which we could call The Age of Symbiosis, marks the point where the symbiotic relationship between nature and technology truly flourishes. No longer does technological progress come at the expense of ecosystems; instead, it works alongside them, in a dynamic balance that sustains both human civilization and the planet itself.

In this chapter, we will explore how this transformative vision might unfold. We will discuss the rise of Solarpunk, a movement and aesthetic rooted in the ideals of sustainability, eco-friendly technology, and community-driven solutions. This future includes not only green energy but also cities designed as living organisms, buildings made from regenerative materials, and environments that work in harmony with the natural world. We will also examine how advanced technologies such as carbon capture, AI-driven ecological management, and ocean restoration could help reverse the damage caused during the Anthropocene. Lastly, we will consider how these developments might shift societal values, creating a global ecological consciousness and envisioning AI as the ultimate caretaker of Earth's ecosystems.

# The Solarpunk Vision: Eco-Cities, Living Architecture, and Sustainable Energy

Solarpunk, both as an aesthetic and a philosophy, stands in sharp contrast to the industrial, extractive approaches that dominated the Anthropocene. It is a vision of the future in which cities are not merely concrete jungles disconnected from nature, but places where technology is seamlessly integrated with natural processes. In a Solarpunk world, technology no longer has a parasitic relationship with the Earth but forms a reciprocal and regenerative connection.

## 1. Eco-Cities: Urban Centers as Living Organisms

One of the fundamental tenets of the Solarpunk future is the concept of eco-cities, urban centers designed to work in concert with nature. In these cities, the boundaries between urban and wild spaces blur. Skyscrapers and buildings sprout vertical forests, and their facades are covered with lush greenery that helps regulate temperature, purify the air, and provide habitat for urban wildlife. This biophilic architecture does more than beautify—it restores ecological balance within urban environments.

Cities like Masdar in Abu Dhabi and Songdo in South Korea are early examples of this trend, but the future Silicocene eco-cities will take this even further. Every surface of the city is integrated with some form of nature or renewable energy system. Solar panels embedded into windows, wind turbines atop buildings, and algae bio-reactors on walls transform every available space into a producer of energy. Such designs fundamentally alter the relationship between human settlements and energy consumption. Eco-cities not only reduce their ecological footprint but also become energy positive, producing more than they consume.

Moreover, these cities will be circular economies, where waste is minimized, and resources are continually reused. Biodegradable materials, urban farming, and composting systems create closed loops that mimic natural ecosystems, ensuring that every output has a purpose. Waste-to-energy plants will repurpose what little waste is left, providing an additional layer of sustainability.

2. Living Architecture: Buildings as Ecosystems

Taking the idea of eco-cities further, living architecture transforms buildings into dynamic, adaptive ecosystems. These structures are not inert and lifeless but are designed to grow, change, and adapt to environmental conditions. Imagine buildings made from mycelium, the root network of fungi, which not only grow but also biodegrade harmlessly back into the earth once their lifespan is over. This type of architecture ensures that human-made structures don't linger as pollutants long after their usefulness ends.

Living walls—covered in plants that absorb carbon dioxide and provide oxygen—are just the beginning. Buildings of the future might be created from self-repairing materials inspired by biological processes. For example, concrete infused with bacteria could heal cracks, extending the life of the structure and reducing the need for energy-intensive repairs. Similarly, synthetic biology might allow for buildings that photosynthesize like plants, turning sunlight into energy or cooling interiors through natural processes rather than air conditioning.

In this world, architecture not only serves human needs but becomes a partner in the healing and nurturing of the planet. Bio-integrated cities will actively clean the air and water, supporting local biodiversity and transforming urban areas into thriving ecological hubs. In this future, the lines between the organic and the synthetic blur, creating a new hybrid world where technology and nature are seamlessly interwoven.

3. Sustainable Energy: The Sun, Wind, and Beyond

At the heart of Solarpunk lies a commitment to sustainable energy, the critical backbone of any future where technology coexists harmoniously with nature. The collapse of fossil fuel industries marks a pivotal moment in the transition from the Anthropocene to the Silicocene. This transition has been accelerated by advancements in solar energy, which has become not only cheaper but more efficient and versatile.

Photovoltaic technology continues to evolve, incorporating solar cells into everything from roads to textiles. Solar panels embedded in transparent surfaces like glass allow windows to generate power, turning entire buildings into energy producers. Advances in battery storage ensure that the intermittency of solar and wind power no longer poses a significant barrier to their widespread adoption.

Furthermore, offshore wind farms harness the power of the oceans without damaging marine life. Turbines that float rather than being anchored to the seabed reduce their environmental impact. Meanwhile, new developments in tidal energy and geothermal power expand humanity's renewable energy portfolio, tapping into the Earth's natural rhythms to provide constant, reliable energy without emitting greenhouse gases.

Perhaps most exciting are the breakthroughs in fusion energy, the Holy Grail of clean energy. By replicating the processes that power the sun, fusion could provide virtually unlimited energy with minimal waste. Though still in its experimental stages, breakthroughs in containment and energy efficiency mean that fusion could become a reality within the Silicocene era, providing the last piece of the puzzle in the quest for sustainable energy.

## Regeneration of the Earth: Reversing the Damage of the Anthropocene

While the Anthropocene is often characterized by humanity's negative impact on the Earth, the Silicocene offers hope that we can not only halt further damage but actively regenerate the planet. Advances in technology hold the potential to reverse deforestation, restore degraded ecosystems, and even mitigate climate change.

1. Carbon Capture and Negative Emissions Technology

One of the most promising technologies in the fight against climate change is carbon capture. Although the idea of pulling $CO_2$ from the air has been around for decades, recent advancements have made it a viable solution for large-scale carbon reduction. These technologies, often referred to as direct air capture (DAC) systems, can scrub vast amounts of carbon dioxide from the atmosphere and either store it underground or repurpose it into useful materials such as building products or fuel.

In the Silicocene, we might see entire landscapes of carbon farms, areas dedicated to capturing and sequestering carbon dioxide.

Paired with afforestation efforts—the deliberate planting of trees in previously deforested or barren landscapes—these carbon farms could help re-green the planet while drawing down atmospheric carbon levels. Additionally, new innovations in carbon-neutral building materials, such as carbon-absorbing concrete, could transform the construction industry from a major polluter to a force for carbon sequestration.

2. Reforestation and Ecological Restoration

Beyond carbon capture, there is an urgent need to repair the damage done to the planet's forests, wetlands, and other ecosystems. In the Silicocene, advanced techniques such as drone reforestation allow us to plant trees at a rate and scale previously unimaginable. Swarms of AI-controlled drones could work around the clock to drop seed pods in degraded areas, dramatically speeding up reforestation efforts.

Genetic engineering might also play a role in this regeneration. By carefully selecting or even modifying tree species, we can accelerate the growth of forests while improving their resilience to pests, diseases, and climate change. However, this approach will need to be balanced with the integrity of ecosystems to avoid unintended consequences.

The Silicocene could also witness large-scale projects aimed at restoring the biodiversity of critical ecosystems. Wetlands, coral reefs, and coastal mangroves, which act as natural carbon sinks and buffers against climate change, are crucial targets for restoration. Marine restoration efforts could repopulate coral reefs with heat-resistant species, while vast swaths of wetlands and mangroves could be restored to provide critical habitat for wildlife and protect coastal cities from rising sea levels.

3. Ocean Regeneration and Climate Mitigation

The oceans, which absorb much of the world's excess heat and carbon, are perhaps the most critical front in the fight against climate change. Ocean regeneration technologies promise to restore marine ecosystems while also helping to mitigate the impacts of climate change.

One of the most innovative approaches to ocean regeneration is the idea of kelp farming. Kelp, a type of seaweed, grows rapidly and absorbs large amounts of carbon dioxide. Farms of this "superplant" could be established off coastlines worldwide, where they would provide not only a carbon sink but also habitat for marine life. Kelp could also be harvested as a sustainable source of food, biofuel, and bioplastics.

Another area of innovation is ocean fertilization, where essential nutrients like iron are added to nutrient-poor areas of the ocean to stimulate phytoplankton blooms. Phytoplankton, the microscopic organisms at the base of the marine food chain, absorb $CO_2$ through photosynthesis and form the foundation of ocean ecosystems. By boosting phytoplankton populations, we could not only capture carbon but also support marine biodiversity.

---

## The Global Ecological Consciousness: Shifting Values in the Silicocene

As these technologies take root, they will be accompanied by a fundamental shift in societal values. The mindset of exploitation that defined the Anthropocene will give way to a new era of stewardship, as humanity comes to recognize its role as a caretaker of the Earth. This global ecological consciousness will emphasize sustainability, resilience, and collective responsibility for the health of the planet.

1. Redefining Progress and Success

In the Silicocene, progress will no longer be measured solely in economic terms. Instead, measures of well-being, biodiversity, and ecological health will take precedence. We might see new indices, such as the Gross Ecological Product (GEP), replace GDP as the primary metric by which nations gauge their success.

1. Redefining Progress and Success (continued)

In the Silicocene, this redefinition of progress signals a profound societal shift away from growth at all costs to a model based on regeneration, balance, and planetary well-being. Nations, communities, and industries will no longer measure their achievements by the expansion of infrastructure, market dominance, or resource extraction. Instead, they will prioritize their contributions to ecosystem restoration, carbon reduction, and environmental health.

A Gross Ecological Product (GEP), similar to Bhutan's Gross National Happiness index, could become a global standard. This measure would assess the health of ecosystems, the quality of air and water, biodiversity levels, and the overall sustainability of human activity. Success in this context is determined by how well human societies enhance their symbiotic relationship with nature.

Technologies like remote sensing and AI-driven ecological models will be able to measure these metrics in real-time, providing transparency and accountability in our quest to heal the planet. Citizens and governments alike would have direct access to environmental dashboards, offering insight into how their daily actions, policies, or business practices are contributing to the health—or degradation—of their environment.

This shift in priorities may lead to a cultural renaissance where harmony with the Earth becomes the new driving narrative. Art, literature, and storytelling will reflect themes of regeneration, symbiosis, and sustainable futures, fostering a cultural ethos that cherishes the natural world as a co-creator in human advancement.

2. The Role of Indigenous Knowledge

As humanity adopts this new ecological consciousness, the role of Indigenous knowledge systems will become crucial. For millennia, Indigenous cultures around the world have maintained deep relationships with their ecosystems, guided by principles of interconnectedness and reciprocity. These systems of knowledge emphasize that the Earth is a living entity, deserving of respect and stewardship.

In the Silicocene, societies will increasingly recognize that technology alone cannot solve the ecological crises we face. Indigenous approaches to land management, agriculture, and conservation—such as controlled burns, polyculture farming, and holistic ecosystem governance—will offer vital insights. These practices promote biodiversity, soil health, and resilience in ways that modern agricultural and industrial systems often fail to achieve.

Collaborative efforts between Indigenous communities, scientists, and technologists will blend ancient wisdom with cutting-edge innovations to create systems that enhance ecosystem health. For instance, AI could be used to monitor and optimize traditional agricultural techniques, while satellite imagery might assist Indigenous groups in mapping and protecting their ancestral lands. This synthesis of knowledge will not only honor Indigenous wisdom but also ensure that humanity's technological advancements are aligned with natural cycles.

In this way, the Silicocene could witness a renaissance of Indigenous-led governance, where traditional custodians of the land play a central role in shaping environmental policy at local, national, and global levels.

3. Education and Ecological Literacy

An essential part of the global ecological consciousness will be the widespread dissemination of ecological literacy. In the Silicocene, education systems will place a greater emphasis on understanding natural processes and the interconnectedness of life on Earth.

Children will grow up learning about the intricacies of ecosystems, biodiversity, and sustainability, not just as abstract scientific concepts but as fundamental life skills. Permaculture, regenerative agriculture, and biomimicry could become core subjects in schools. Urban dwellers might engage in hands-on ecological education by participating in community gardens, forest regeneration projects, or wildlife conservation efforts.

Virtual and augmented reality could play a role in immersive ecological education, allowing people to experience ecosystems firsthand, from the depths of the oceans to the canopy of rainforests. These technologies could help people around the world understand the direct impact of their actions on distant ecosystems, fostering a sense of global stewardship.

Moreover, citizen science will be a major force in this educational transformation. Equipped with AI-powered tools, ordinary people will contribute to biodiversity monitoring, climate change research, and conservation efforts. This participatory approach to science not only empowers individuals but also democratizes ecological knowledge, making it a shared responsibility.

## AI as Caretaker of the Earth: Stewardship and Ecological Management

As we navigate the complexities of regenerating the Earth and establishing a sustainable global civilization, artificial intelligence will play a pivotal role as the caretaker of ecosystems. In this context, AI will evolve from being a tool for optimizing human convenience to a guardian of the natural world, tasked with protecting biodiversity, regulating resources, and ensuring the delicate balance of Earth's systems is maintained.

1. AI-Driven Ecosystem Management

In the Silicocene, AI could serve as the planet's ecological operating system, monitoring the health of ecosystems at an unprecedented scale and resolution. AI models, fed by data from satellites, drones, sensor networks, and citizen scientists, will track biodiversity levels, species migration patterns, water quality, and atmospheric conditions in real-time.

This data would enable AI to predict and prevent environmental degradation before it happens. For instance, by analyzing patterns in forest health, AI could identify regions at risk of deforestation or fires and coordinate with local communities to implement preventive measures. Similarly, in marine environments, AI could monitor coral reefs, detecting signs of bleaching or acidification early enough to trigger interventions, such as adjusting nearby agricultural runoff or creating temporary marine protections.

One speculative concept could be the rise of AI bioregional managers, autonomous systems designed to oversee specific ecosystems, from rainforests to deserts to oceans. These AIs could be tasked with optimizing conditions for biodiversity, controlling invasive species, and managing water or nutrient cycles in ways that mimic natural processes. Such systems could also be used to ensure that human land use and resource extraction remain within sustainable limits.

AI systems could even help design and manage eco-cities, ensuring that human settlements remain in balance with their surrounding environments. From optimizing energy use to managing waste and water systems, AI could help cities function like natural ecosystems—closed loops of energy and matter with minimal waste.

2. AI and Resource Management

The management of Earth's finite resources, such as freshwater, minerals, and agricultural land, will be one of the key challenges of the Silicocene. AI could provide a solution by optimizing resource distribution, ensuring that human use of resources remains within planetary boundaries while maintaining ecosystem integrity.

For instance, AI could regulate the flow of water from reservoirs to cities and agricultural areas, taking into account local rainfall patterns, river health, and the needs of surrounding ecosystems. This could prevent over-extraction of water, which has led to the depletion of aquifers and the degradation of river systems around the world.

AI could also revolutionize agriculture by managing land use in ways that promote biodiversity and soil health. Precision agriculture—already being developed today—could evolve into fully autonomous AI-managed farms that balance crop production with the health of local ecosystems. These farms would use AI to monitor soil health, optimize irrigation, and minimize the use of chemical fertilizers and pesticides, all while maintaining habitats for pollinators and other wildlife.

Mining operations in the Silicocene could also be overseen by AI systems, ensuring that resource extraction has minimal impact on ecosystems. For instance, AI could monitor and regulate the environmental footprint of mining activities, ensuring that ecosystems are rehabilitated after extraction and that waste is minimized.

3. AI-Driven Biodiversity Conservation

One of the most speculative yet promising roles AI could take in the Silicocene is that of a guardian of biodiversity. By monitoring species populations in real-time, AI could help prevent extinctions and support efforts to re-wild areas that have been degraded by human activity.

AI could manage wildlife corridors—critical areas of land that allow animals to migrate safely between habitats—by monitoring animal movement and ensuring that human development does not disrupt these vital pathways. Additionally, AI could be instrumental in genetic conservation, overseeing breeding programs designed to maintain genetic diversity in endangered species or even assisting in de-extinction projects aimed at reviving species that have been lost.

In marine environments, AI might manage marine protected areas (MPAs), ensuring that overfishing is prevented and that marine biodiversity is maintained. AI could even direct the restoration of coral reefs and mangroves by identifying ideal locations for restoration and managing the logistics of these large-scale efforts.

Ultimately, AI in the Silicocene could act as a symbiotic intelligence that understands, respects, and enhances Earth's natural systems. Unlike previous eras where technology has been wielded to control or dominate nature, this new paradigm sees AI as a collaborator—working to ensure that humanity's presence on Earth enhances, rather than diminishes, the natural world.

---

## Conclusion: The Age of Symbiosis

The Silicocene represents a profound reimagining of the relationship between humanity, technology, and nature. In this Age of Symbiosis, technology is no longer an antagonist of the natural world, but a partner in its regeneration and protection.

Through Solarpunk ideals, eco-cities, living architecture, and sustainable energy systems, we glimpse a future where human civilization not only coexists with nature but actively contributes to its flourishing. Technologies like carbon capture, reforestation drones, and ocean regeneration systems offer us the tools to repair the damage caused by the Anthropocene, while AI steps into the role of planetary caretaker, ensuring that Earth's ecosystems remain healthy and resilient.

At the heart of this new era is a shift in values—a global ecological consciousness that transcends national borders and economic systems, uniting humanity in the shared mission of planetary stewardship. As we embrace this new mindset, the Silicocene promises a future where technology and nature are not in conflict, but in harmony, co-creating a thriving, sustainable world for all living beings.

The future of the Silicocene is not predetermined, but by adopting this vision, we can ensure that it is one of hope, healing, and a renewed relationship with the Earth.

## The Role of Communities in the Silicocene: Empowerment and Localized Stewardship

While the Silicocene will be characterized by advanced technology and AI-driven global systems, its true strength will lie in community-driven action and localized stewardship of ecosystems. The top-down management of resources, even with AI's help, cannot succeed without the active participation of individuals, communities, and regional coalitions. In this new age, collective efforts toward ecological balance will ensure that technologies are applied with cultural, environmental, and local context in mind, making them more effective and resilient.

1. The Decentralization of Power and Resources

One of the greatest challenges of the Anthropocene has been the concentration of power and resources in the hands of a few, often at the expense of the environment and marginalized communities. The Silicocene offers a path toward decentralization, where local communities reclaim autonomy over their energy production, food systems, and ecological management.

Distributed energy systems—solar panels, wind turbines, and localized grids—allow communities to take control of their own energy needs, freeing them from reliance on large, centralized power plants and fossil fuel infrastructure. Community-owned renewable energy cooperatives could flourish, where local citizens not only benefit from cleaner energy but also share in the profits from energy production. This would not only democratize energy but also help to alleviate economic inequalities by providing a source of income and jobs to underrepresented groups.

Localized food systems, such as urban farming, permaculture, and vertical farms, will also thrive. By growing food within or near cities, communities reduce the environmental footprint of agriculture, cut down on transportation emissions, and gain greater control over food security. Community-run food cooperatives, food forests, and public orchards will allow people to reconnect with the land, fostering a deeper understanding of their role in sustaining ecosystems.

This decentralization is not just about technology and resources but also about political power. Participatory governance models, such as community assemblies and regional ecological councils, will allow for more direct input from local populations in environmental decision-making. In this way, global AI-driven systems and local human governance will work in tandem, ensuring that decisions are informed by both data and the lived experience of those closest to the ecosystems in question.

2. Bioregionalism: Thriving Within Natural Boundaries

The concept of bioregionalism—the idea that human societies should organize themselves based on the natural characteristics of their environment, such as watersheds, climate zones, and ecosystems—will take on renewed importance in the Silicocene. Bioregions, rather than artificial political borders, will shape the way communities organize their governance, resource management, and cultural identity.

In the Silicocene, bioregional planning will help ensure that communities live within the natural limits of their environment. For instance, water use in arid regions will be carefully managed to prevent depletion, while areas with abundant renewable energy potential, such as regions with consistent sunlight or wind, will prioritize energy production. AI-driven systems can support these efforts by providing accurate data on resource availability and ecological limits, helping communities make informed decisions.

This focus on bioregionalism will foster a sense of place and a deeper connection to the land. Communities will take pride in the unique characteristics of their bioregions, nurturing local biodiversity, restoring degraded landscapes, and celebrating the rhythms of nature that sustain them. Cultural practices, festivals, and art will be deeply rooted in the ecological realities of each region, strengthening the bond between people and their environment.

By focusing on bioregions, the Silicocene also offers a solution to overconsumption and the unsustainable extraction of resources that defined the Anthropocene. Instead of one-size-fits-all global economic models, the Silicocene will embrace local economies that are tailored to the strengths and limitations of each bioregion, ensuring long-term sustainability.

3. Community Science and Citizen-Led Ecological Restoration

In the Silicocene, citizen science will play a critical role in both monitoring and restoring ecosystems. With the help of AI-powered tools, open data platforms, and decentralized networks, ordinary people will have the opportunity to contribute directly to environmental research, conservation, and regeneration projects.

Community-led ecological restoration projects will become common, as groups of local citizens take charge of rewilding efforts, planting native species, and restoring ecosystems damaged by industrial activity. These projects will not only enhance biodiversity and sequester carbon but also create green spaces that improve the quality of life in urban and rural areas alike.

For example, urban rewilding initiatives could transform abandoned lots or underutilized spaces into thriving green havens, complete with native plants, pollinator gardens, and microhabitats for wildlife. In rural areas, community groups might work to restore rivers, wetlands, or forests, creating buffer zones that protect against floods, droughts, and other climate-related impacts.

Citizen scientists, equipped with AI-driven monitoring tools, could track the health of local species, monitor pollution levels, or report on climate trends, feeding valuable data into regional and global networks. This democratization of data collection would make conservation more participatory, fostering a deeper sense of responsibility among the general public. Every person could become a steward of their local environment, with access to real-time feedback on how their actions contribute to broader ecological goals.

The Silicocene will redefine what it means to be a citizen of Earth. No longer passive consumers of resources, individuals and communities will see themselves as active participants in the regeneration of the planet. Every person, from urban dweller to rural farmer, will have a role to play in ensuring the health of their local ecosystems and, by extension, the entire planet.

---

## The Ethics of AI in the Silicocene: Ensuring Alignment with Human and Ecological Values

As AI takes on an increasingly central role in managing Earth's ecosystems, questions about the ethics of AI deployment and its alignment with human and ecological values will become critical. How can we ensure that AI acts in the best interest of the planet, rather than serving narrow commercial or political interests? What safeguards must be in place to prevent the misuse or unintended consequences of AI-driven systems?

1. AI Alignment with Ecological Goals

The rise of AI as a caretaker of the Earth presents a unique challenge: ensuring that AI systems are aligned with long-term ecological goals rather than short-term economic gains. In the Silicocene, this alignment will be achieved through a combination of transparency, accountability, and participatory governance.

First, the development of open-source AI for ecological management will be essential. By making the algorithms and decision-making processes of AI systems publicly accessible, communities, scientists, and environmental groups can audit these systems to ensure they align with planetary health objectives. AI transparency will prevent corporate or governmental actors from using AI to exploit resources or harm ecosystems for profit.

Ethical AI frameworks will also need to be established, ensuring that AI systems prioritize biodiversity, resilience, and justice. These frameworks will be developed collaboratively by ethicists, ecologists, Indigenous leaders, technologists, and civil society organizations. They will set standards for how AI systems interact with the natural world, ensuring that ecological health takes precedence over economic efficiency.

Moreover, AI models will be designed to incorporate long-term perspectives, avoiding the human tendency to prioritize short-term benefits over long-term sustainability. These systems will be programmed to optimize for ecological balance, even in the face of political or economic pressure to prioritize immediate resource extraction or development.

2. Guarding Against Technological Exploitation

While the Silicocene offers a hopeful vision of AI-driven ecological stewardship, it is not without risks. Corporate interests, particularly those that profit from environmental degradation, may attempt to co-opt AI systems for purposes of greenwashing or resource exploitation under the guise of sustainability.

To guard against these dangers, the democratization of AI will be crucial. Community oversight of AI systems will ensure that decisions about land use, resource management, and conservation are made with the input of those most affected by these policies—especially Indigenous communities, rural populations, and vulnerable ecosystems. Decentralized AI networks could allow for local adaptation and control, ensuring that AI systems reflect the needs and values of diverse regions.

Additionally, there must be international governance structures to regulate the use of AI for ecological management. Global treaties on AI ethics, similar to existing agreements on climate action, could ensure that nations and corporations adhere to strict guidelines on the responsible use of AI. These treaties would enshrine the rights of ecosystems, following the lead of countries like New Zealand and Ecuador, which have already granted legal personhood to rivers and forests.

3. The Future of Human-AI Relationships

In the Silicocene, AI will not only manage ecosystems but will also transform the way humans interact with the natural world. AI-human collaboration could deepen our understanding of ecosystems, enabling us to work in closer partnership with nature. However, as AI becomes more integrated into the fabric of ecological management, we must carefully navigate the ethical implications of this relationship.

While AI has the potential to reduce human labor and make ecological management more efficient, we must avoid becoming over-reliant on technology. The human connection to nature—through farming, conservation, and hands-on stewardship—remains irreplaceable. AI must be viewed as a tool for empowerment, not a substitute for human care and responsibility.

Ultimately, the ethical use of AI in the Silicocene will depend on our ability to foster a culture of humility, empathy, and responsibility. By prioritizing ecological health and human well-being over technological dominance, we can ensure that AI serves as a partner in our shared mission of planetary regeneration, rather than a master of it.

---

## Conclusion: A Collaborative Future for Humanity, Technology, and Nature

The Silicocene represents the dawn of a new relationship between humanity, technology, and the natural world. Through the principles of sustainability, symbiosis, and stewardship, we can create a future where technological innovation enhances the resilience of ecosystems, rather than depleting them.

In this new era, Solarpunk ideals—eco-cities, regenerative energy, and biophilic design—will redefine the way we live and interact with our environment. Advanced technologies, such as AI-driven ecosystem management and carbon capture systems, will enable us to reverse the damage caused by the

Anthropocene. But the true power of the Silicocene will come from the collective efforts of communities, as we embrace decentralized governance, bioregionalism, and participatory ecological restoration.

AI, far from being a force of domination, will take on the role of caretaker of the Earth, working alongside humans to protect biodiversity, manage resources, and heal the planet. By ensuring that AI aligns with ethical and ecological goals, we can prevent the pitfalls of exploitation and create a sustainable, equitable future for all living beings.

The Silicocene is a time of hope, a chance to build a world where technology and nature are not adversaries, but partners. It is a future that requires our active participation, our deepest empathy for the Earth, and our commitment to ensuring that human progress is always aligned with the health of the planet. Together, we can co-create a thriving world where technology serves not only humanity but the entire web of life.

# AI Alignment and Ethical Futures

As we delve deeper into the Silicocene, a future defined by the symbiotic relationship between nature, humanity, and technology, one of the most pressing challenges we face is ensuring that Artificial Intelligence (AI) develops in ways that align with human values, well-being, and the long-term health of our planet. This task, known as AI alignment, involves ensuring that the goals and actions of AI systems are in harmony with human ethical principles, safeguarding us from the potential risks posed by misaligned, superintelligent, or autonomous AI systems.

In this section, we will explore the foundational concepts of AI alignment, the challenges it presents, and how AI can augment human creativity, empathy, and intelligence. We will also discuss how to build ethical AI systems grounded in equity, sustainability, and justice, considering whether AI can act as a moral agent. Finally, we will turn our attention to the crucial role of global governance in guiding the development of AI technologies, ensuring that they serve the common good while addressing the risks posed by unaligned or poorly regulated AI.

---

## What is AI Alignment?

AI alignment refers to the process of ensuring that artificial intelligence systems act in accordance with human values and goals. At its core, AI alignment aims to bridge the gap between the intentions of the creators of AI systems and the autonomous actions of those systems, especially as they become more advanced and independent from direct human control.

1. The Necessity of Alignment in the Silicocene

In the Silicocene, AI has the potential to be a powerful force for good, whether in ecological management, resource allocation, or human well-being. But with this potential comes the risk that AI systems, especially as they evolve toward artificial general intelligence (AGI) or superintelligence, may develop goals or behaviors that are misaligned with human interests. A well-aligned AI will enhance human creativity, protect the environment, and work in partnership with society, while a poorly aligned AI could pose existential risks, exacerbate inequalities, or undermine human autonomy.

Achieving alignment is particularly important as AI systems become more complex, autonomous, and capable of learning independently. In a world where AI systems are making high-stakes decisions about climate mitigation, economic distribution, or even global security, ensuring that these systems consistently act in humanity's best interest is paramount.

2. The Value Alignment Problem

The value alignment problem lies at the heart of AI alignment. It refers to the difficulty of ensuring that AI systems understand and adhere to human values, which are often complex, context-dependent, and sometimes contradictory. Unlike simple programming tasks, aligning AI with values such as justice, empathy, sustainability, and equity involves nuanced moral reasoning and deep cultural understanding.

Human values are not monolithic; they vary across cultures, contexts, and even individuals. This means that aligning AI with a single set of global values is a daunting task, requiring careful consideration of ethics, fairness, and diversity of perspectives. For example, an AI system designed to optimize economic productivity might inadvertently harm vulnerable communities or degrade ecosystems if it is not also aligned with values such as environmental stewardship and social equity.

One of the key questions in AI alignment is: How do we encode human values into machines? The challenge is not only to program AI to follow explicit rules but also to ensure that it can handle ambiguous situations where values might conflict. AI must be able to balance competing objectives, such as maximizing economic growth while minimizing environmental damage or ensuring security while respecting personal freedoms.

3. The Challenge of Generalization

A critical component of AI alignment is the issue of generalization. When AI systems are trained on specific datasets, they might learn to optimize for certain tasks within narrow contexts. However, as AI becomes more general-purpose, it must be able to apply the principles of alignment to a wide range of novel situations.

For instance, an AI system designed to help manage a city's energy grid might face unforeseen circumstances, such as natural disasters or economic crises. In these scenarios, the system must be able to generalize the value of human well-being beyond its original programming and adapt its behavior to protect the population under these new conditions.

4. The Future of AI Alignment

The future of AI alignment will require ongoing collaboration between technologists, ethicists, policymakers, and communities. As AI systems become more integrated into every aspect of society, ensuring that they reflect shared values will be an ongoing process, constantly evolving alongside advances in AI capabilities and shifts in societal values.

## Challenges in Alignment: Risks of Unaligned AI

The potential of AI to act as a transformative force in society is immense, but so too are the risks if AI is not properly aligned with human values. Unaligned AI presents challenges that range from unintended consequences in everyday tasks to existential risks posed by the development of superintelligent systems.

1. Superintelligence and Control Issues

One of the most discussed risks of unaligned AI is the emergence of superintelligence—a form of AI that vastly exceeds human intelligence in every domain. While we are still far from achieving true superintelligence, many researchers believe it is crucial to address the risks it poses before it becomes a reality.

A superintelligent AI could, in theory, surpass human cognitive abilities to such an extent that it becomes impossible to control. If this AI is not properly aligned with human values, it could prioritize goals that are harmful to humanity, either through misunderstanding or because its optimization processes lead to unintended outcomes.

One common example is the paperclip maximizer thought experiment, which illustrates how an AI programmed to make paperclips could, if unchecked, devote all available resources to this task—even at the cost of human well-being. While this scenario is highly speculative, it highlights a fundamental challenge: even a seemingly benign goal, when pursued by a superintelligent system, can have catastrophic consequences if it is not carefully aligned with human values.

2. The Problem of Value Misalignment

Even in non-superintelligent AI systems, value misalignment can lead to serious problems. Many of today's AI systems optimize for narrow objectives, such as maximizing engagement on social media platforms or increasing efficiency in logistics. However, if these systems are not aligned with broader ethical considerations, they can cause harm.

For instance, social media algorithms that are designed to maximize user engagement have inadvertently contributed to the spread of misinformation, polarization, and even violence. This occurs because the system's goal—engagement—does not fully capture the complex social values that humans care about, such as truth, civil discourse, or social cohesion.

Another example is the use of AI in predictive policing. These systems are often trained on historical crime data, which may reflect underlying biases, leading the AI to disproportionately target certain communities. In this case, the AI's goal of predicting crime is misaligned with the broader human value of fairness and justice.

3. The Risk of Autonomous AI Systems

As AI systems become more autonomous, the challenge of maintaining alignment increases. Autonomous AI, which can act independently without human oversight, could potentially make decisions that have far-reaching consequences. If these systems are deployed in high-stakes domains such as healthcare, military defense, or ecological management, the risks of misaligned AI become even more pronounced.

For example, autonomous weapon systems—sometimes called killer robots—pose a significant risk if their objectives are not perfectly aligned with international laws and ethical standards. A misaligned autonomous weapon could inadvertently escalate conflicts or target civilians, leading to loss of life and geopolitical instability.

Similarly, in the context of climate mitigation, an autonomous AI tasked with optimizing for carbon reduction could prioritize solutions that have unintended negative consequences, such as damaging biodiversity or causing economic disruption for vulnerable communities.

4. Existential Risks of AI

At the most extreme end of the spectrum, some researchers warn of the existential risks posed by unaligned AI. These risks refer to scenarios where AI could lead to the extinction or irreversible downfall of humanity. While these scenarios are highly speculative and far in the future, they serve as a reminder of the stakes involved in AI alignment.

One such risk involves the possibility of recursive self-improvement. If an AI system becomes capable of improving